The Britisl of the Napoleonic Period
1800–15
History, Organisation and Equipment

GABRIELE ESPOSITO

HISTORIC ARMIES SERIES, VOLUME 3

Title page image: Non-commissioned officer (NCO) of the 23rd Regiment of Foot. (Photo by Carwyn Balch, copyright by 23rd Regiment of Foot, The Royal Welch Fusileers 1809–1815)

Contents page image: Officer of the Light Dragoons wearing M1796 uniform and M1812 shako. (ASKB)

Back cover image: Drum and flag of the 32nd Regiment of Foot. (Photo and copyright by 32nd Cornwall Regiment of Foot)

The author

Gabriele Esposito is a military historian who works as a freelance author and researcher in the military history sector. He is an expert specialising in uniformology and his interests and expertise range from ancient civilisations to modern post-colonial conflicts. In recent years, he has conducted research on the military history of non-European countries. His books and essays are published regularly by international publishers. He is also the author of numerous military history articles appearing in specialised magazines.

Acknowledgements

This book is dedicated to my beloved parents, Maria Rosaria and Benedetto. A very special mention goes to the brilliant reenactment groups that collaborated allowing their photographs to be included in this book. Without the incredible research of their members, this publication would not be the same. I want to express my deep gratitude to the following living history associations: 1/95th Rifles Living History Society, 23rd Regiment of Foot (The Royal Welch Fusiliers 1809-1815), 2nd Battalion 95th Rifles, 32nd Cornwall Regiment of Foot, 44th East Essex Regiment of Foot, Gordons Living History, His Majesty's 33rd Regiment of Foot, King's German Legion Artillery, Old 68th Society, and the 79th Cameron Highlanders.

Published by Key Books
An imprint of Key Publishing Ltd
PO Box 100
Stamford
Lincs PE9 1XQ

www.keypublishing.com

The rights of Gabriele Esposito to be identified as the author of this book has been asserted in accordance with the Copyright, Designs and Patents Act 1988 Sections 77 and 78.

Copyright © Gabriele Esposito, 2023

ISBN 978 1 80282 601 2

Typeset by SJmagic DESIGN SERVICES, India.

Contents

Introduction

This book presents a detailed overview of the organisation, uniforms and arms of the British Army during the Napoleonic Wars. The period represents one of the most glorious moments in the military history of Britain, during which the British Army fought around the globe to contain the expansionist ambitions of the great French commander and political leader Napoleon Bonaparte (1768–1821) and his newly established French Empire. After the 1802 Treaty of Amiens, which ended hostilities between Britain and France, was broken in 1803, Great Britain resumed war with its old enemy, this time led by the ambitious Napoleon. Napoleon was the greatest military commander of his times and transformed the French Army into the most lethal fighting machine of the early 19th century.

The British war experience of 1793–1803 had not been a positive one. The Army was still recovering from the crushing defeats it suffered during the American War of Independence (1775–83) and badly needed reforming to become a more efficient and modern fighting force. At the turn of the new century, Great Britain was the greatest colonial power in the world with the most formidable navy, yet its army was too weak to confront the French on equal terms. The British land forces lacked a great leader and their methods were still influenced by outdated tactical models. During the Napoleonic Wars, the British military apparatus did its best to improve, guided by a new generation of intelligent officers. These innovative and capable men reformed the British Army by improving its standards of service and by creating a new relationship, based on mutual trust, with the men under their command.

Arthur Wellesley (1769–1852), 1st Duke of Wellington, was the greatest of these officers and one of the few European generals who could effectively counter Napoleon. It was Wellington who forged the new British Army, by fighting against the French in the Iberian Peninsula during 1808–14. During 1800–15, British officers reformed the tactical and operational patterns of their units in entirety. In fact, a light infantry revolution took place among the ranks of the foot troops. During this experimental process, tactics were under review as officers searched for the most expedient methods with the most effective results. The glorious actions of the British Army at the Peninsula were not the only battles fought during this time, however. There were three campaigns conducted in the Netherlands (1799, 1809 and 1814), which were disastrous for the British Army.

To follow the evolution of the British Army, I have divided the text in this book into 10 chapters. The first reviews the elite of the British infantry – the three regiments of Foot Guards; the second chapter analyses the general organisation of the 104 regiments of line infantry serving during the Napoleonic Wars; the third chapter assesses the Highland troops, with their many distinctive features; the fourth chapter focuses on light infantry and the important light infantry revolution mentioned above. Chapter five examines the elite of the British cavalry – the three regiments of Life Guards and Horse Guards; chapter six scrutinises the general organisation of the heavy cavalry, with its regiments of Dragoon Guards and Dragoons, while the seventh chapter provides an overview of light cavalry. Chapter eight investigates the 'foreign' troops serving in the British Army during the Napoleonic Wars. The final two chapters appraise the Royal Artillery and other specialist corps of the British Army, as well as the uniforms of the regiments.

Chapter 1

The Foot Guards

All the European armies of the early 19th century had guard units, which were an elite corps in the military forces of each country. These could be, for example, a small bodyguard corps, whose main function was to escort the monarchy, or larger combatant units with superior training. In Great Britain, the Royal Guard had a very long tradition and consisted of units with 'special' status that performed specific duties. The infantry component of the Royal Guard consisted of three regiments: the 1st Foot Guards (Grenadier Guards), the 2nd Foot Guards (Coldstream Guards), and the 3rd Foot Guards (Scots Guards). Each of these three infantry units has its own history, from which the names of the corps are derived.

The 1st Foot Guards (Grenadier Guards)

The 1st Foot Guards were created in 1665, by merging two infantry regiments that already had guard status and duties. Lord Wentworth's Regiment had been raised in 1656 by the future King Charles II (1630–1685) during his exile in the Spanish Netherlands (present day Belgium). Initially it consisted of professional soldiers who had followed the future monarch in his exile and who were loyal to the Stuarts (the first monarchs to preside over a kingdom that included Scotland and England). With the Restoration of the monarchy in 1660, the guard unit returned to England to became part of the reorganised English Army. John Russell's Regiment was created in 1660, upon Charles II's return from exile in the Spanish Netherlands. It mirrored the functions and structure of Lord Wentworth's Regiment. In 1665, the two guard regiments were merged into a single unit, and it received the new denomination of 1st Regiment of Foot Guards. The new unit adopted the name Grenadier Guards in 1815, following a Royal Proclamation that transformed the regiment into a grenadier corps. From the late 17th century, the military units defined as grenadiers (heavy infantry) enjoy superior status. This denomination was a heavy infantry corps with special training and equipment.

During the Napoleonic Wars, the French grenadiers of Napoleon's Imperial Guard became the most famous heavy infantrymen in the world, due to their courage and discipline. When they were defeated at Waterloo by the British 1st Foot Guards, the British unit was honoured with the new title Grenadier Guards, and it remains to this day. So, until 1815, the 1st Foot Guards was a line infantry unit (albeit with guard status) and not a grenadier unit.

The 2nd Foot Guards (Coldstream Guards)

The 2nd Foot Guards was created in 1650, as one of the infantry regiments that made up statesman Oliver Cromwell's (1599–1658) New Model Army. Initially known as Monck's Regiment of Foot, in 1660 it supported the Restoration of the Stuart monarchy and made an epic march of five weeks' duration from Coldstream in Berwickshire to London in order to sustain Charles II. It soon acquired the name Coldstream Guards after the village from where the elite infantrymen marched. Following the Restoration of the monarchy, the regiment remained in London to keep order in the capital. In 1661, it received the new official denomination The Lord General's Regiment of Foot Guards. Although the 2nd Foot Guards' unit was older than the 1st Foot Guards, it was placed second in seniority in the Household Troops because it had entered royal service after the Grenadier Guards. Until 1661, it had been part of the New Model Army and not a royal corps. To emphasise that this corps, placed second, was older than the 1st Foot Guard unit, members of the Coldstream Guards adopted a new regimental motto 'Nulli Secundus' (meaning 'second to none'). In 1670, the unit adopted its definitive denomination of Coldstream Regiment of Foot Guards.

The 3rd Foot Guards (Scots Guards)

The 3rd Foot Guards was the oldest of the three guard regiments, but the last to enter English royal service, so it was placed as the third senior unit of the Household Troops. The regiment had been created in 1642, as part of the Scottish Army. Until 1707, the Scottish military forces remained independent from their English equivalent since England and Scotland were two autonomous kingdoms. Charles I, as King of Scotland, ordered the formation of what was to become the 3rd Foot Guards in order to face the Irish Rebellion of 1641. The unit was raised by the Marquis of Argyll, Archibald Campbell, so its first denomination was Marquis of Argyll's Royal Regiment. In 1650, when Charles II became King of Scotland following the execution of his father, the unit acquired guard status and adopted the new title of Lyfe Guard of Foot. In 1651, following Cromwell's victories over the supporters of Charles II, the Scottish Guards were disbanded. They were re-formed ten years later, after Charles II was restored to the English and Scottish thrones. On the establishment of the English Army, this Scottish Regiment of Foot Guards was later transferred (in 1686) to became part of the English Royal Guard albeit a Scots corps. England and Scotland were united in a single state in 1707, and in 1712 the Scots Guards were given their final denomination of 3rd Regiment of Foot Guards.

Officer of the Grenadier Guards in 1815. (ASKB)

Unit organisation 1803

At the beginning of the Napoleonic Wars (1803–15), the three regiments of Foot Guards each had different internal compositions. The 1st Regiment comprised three battalions and was larger than the other two, which had only two battalions each. The Grenadier Guards had received its third battalion in 1760, since it was the senior corps of the Household Troops and also because it had been originally formed by melding two independent infantry regiments. The internal composition of the single battalions was prescribed by official regulations introduced in 1792. Each battalion consisted of ten companies: one of grenadiers, one of light infantrymen and eight of fusiliers (line infantry). The light infantrymen were considered to be newcomers since their presence in each infantry battalion had become a stable one only after the American War of Independence. During that conflict, the British High Command had learned that on broken terrain some infantrymen with light equipment and trained as skirmishers could be a deadly enemy for any infantry formation marching in close order. As a result of those lessons learned fighting American militiamen, the regulations of 1792 prescribed the presence of one light company in each infantry battalion.

The grenadier company and the light company of each battalion were commonly known as 'flank companies', since they were usually deployed on the flanks of the line companies (which were also known as 'battalion companies'). This disposition on the flanks of the unit was not a casual one, since the grenadiers and the light infantrymen had superior training and better equipment than the fusiliers of the 'centre companies'. As a result, it was common practice to detach the flank companies of several battalions and to assemble them together to form 'ad hoc' temporary battalions of grenadiers and light infantrymen. They were usually employed to perform specific duties, and this happened frequently during the Napoleonic Wars. In theory, each infantry company was to comprise 100 men; as a result, a single battalion was to deploy 1,000 soldiers. In practice, however, these official establishments were usually respected only by the three regiments of Foot Guards and by a few line infantry units.

At war

With the outbreak of war with Revolutionary France in 1792, the Foot Guards were put on a war footing and the first battalions of the three regiments were mobilised. They were assembled to form a mixed unit known as a

Grenadiers of the Guard infantry in 1800.

Guard Brigade, which was deployed to Flanders to fight the French. The three mobilised battalions were soon supplemented by a fourth, which was formed by assembling the grenadier companies of the three Foot Guard regiments. Some time later, a fifth battalion was added, which was formed by assembling all the light companies of the three Foot Guard regiments. As a result, the Guard Brigade in Flanders comprised three standard battalions and two temporary ones. The temporary units were re-formed in 1798 to take part in the British offensive launched against the Netherlands during 1799.

After Napoleon became master of France, the battalions of the Foot Guards served on several different fronts, distinguishing themselves with excellent discipline and training.

Grenadier Guards at War

- In 1806, the **1st Battalion of the Grenadier Guards** was sent to Sicily to counter the French and Neapolitan invasion of the island.
- In 1808, for just a few months, the battalion was sent to the Iberian Peninsula to defend Portugal.
- During the following year, it was dispatched to Walcheren in the Netherlands as part of the British expeditionary force that tried, with little success, to open a 'second front' in Flanders.
- In 1812, the battalion returned to Spain, where it took part in the final phase of the Peninsular War (1807–14), which ended with the occupation of southern France in 1814.
- In 1810, the **2nd Battalion of the Grenadier Guards** was sent to the Iberian Peninsula,
- During 1814, it took part in the military operations conducted by the British Army in the Netherlands.
- In 1815, the unit participated, with great distinction, in the decisive battle of Waterloo.

Grenadier NCO of the 23rd Regiment of Foot. (Photo by Carwyn Balch, copyright by 23rd Regiment of Foot, The Royal Welch Fusileers 1809–1815)

- In 1799, the **3rd Battalion of the Grenadier Guards** took part in the failed Anglo-Russian invasion of the Netherlands, launched that year.
- It was sent to Sicily during 1806.
- In 1808 and 1809, it fought in the Iberian Peninsula, before being transferred to Walcheren in the Netherlands.
- In 1811, the battalion returned to Spain, where it fought in the Peninsular War in 1814.
- During 1815, it participated with distinction in the campaign at Waterloo.

Coldstream Guards at War

- In 1799, the **1st Battalion of the Coldstream Guards** took part in the Dutch campaign and followed this with a role in the Egyptian campaign of the following year.
- From 1809 to 1814, it fought with enormous courage in the Iberian Peninsula and southern France.
- In 1809, the **2nd Battalion of the Coldstream Guards** sent its light companies to Walcheren and then to Spain during the following year.
- In 1815, the whole unit fought during the campaign of Waterloo.

Scots Guards at War

- In 1799, the **1st Battalion of the Scots Guards** was sent to the Netherlands and then to Egypt in 1800.
- In 1809, it went to the Iberian Peninsula, serving under Wellington until 1814.
- In that same year, the **2nd Battalion of the Scots Guards** participated in the invasion of the Netherlands with its flank companies.
- In 1810, it sent three companies to the Iberian Peninsula.
- In 1814, it took part in the military operations conducted by the British Army in the Netherlands.
- In 1815, the battalion participated in the Battle of Waterloo.

The character of the Foot Guards

It's clear that the Foot Guard regiments took part in all the most important military operations conducted by Britain during the Napoleonic Wars. They were not 'parade' bodyguard corps but combatant units, with a level of professionalism unrivalled in Europe. The backbone of the three regiments were the non-commissioned officers (NCO) – the professionals who trained their men. It was their duty to transform young recruits into battle-hardened veterans, and preserve the traditions of their regiment. Obedience, endurance, loyalty and pride were the four key factors behind the elite status of the foot guardsmen. Uniforms and equipment were always to be in perfect order and everything was to be clean, especially when performing guard duties at Windsor or at Saint James's Palace. Most of the common soldiers serving in the Foot Guard regiments came from the militia, so they already had some experience of military life. Under the guidance of the NCOs, however, they rapidly transformed into professionals who were able to face any combat situation. Even more important than the NCOs, however, were the officers who gave the Foot Guard regiments their distinctive character. Most of them came from important aristocratic families with long military traditions. They were known as 'gentlemen's sons'. Wellington called them 'fellows in silk stockings'. Despite their nicknames, however, their military competence was unrivalled. Buying an officer's commission in the guard infantry regiments was extremely costly, so only the young sons of the aristocracy or of the upper middle class could afford it. Daily life, in time of peace, was very expensive for such officers since it was spent in the most prestigious gentlemen's clubs of London and there was a requirement to purchase elegant uniforms and to be part of high society. All the officers of the Foot Guard regiments were extremely loyal to the royal family and considered the example of Republican France to be a great potential menace for the social order of their own country. As a result, they held the staunchest anti-French sentiment.

Grenadier NCO of the 23rd Regiment of Foot. (Photo by Carwyn Balch, copyright by 23rd Regiment of Foot, The Royal Welch Fusileers 1809–1815)

Chapter 2
The Line Infantry

During the Napoleonic period, the British line infantry maintained its internal organisation prescribed by the 1792 regulations, without significant changes. It consisted of regiments with one or two battalions each, and each battalion was structured with ten companies.

Composition of a line infantry battalion

Each battalion had its own headquarters supported by one lieutenant-colonel, two majors, one adjutant, one surgeon, two assistant-surgeons, one quartermaster, one sergeant-major, one staff-sergeant paymaster, one sergeant armourer, one drum major, one corporal pioneer and ten pioneers.

Each of these had precise administrative/combat functions and the roles were fundamental to the correct functioning of the battalion. The pioneers including their corporal were to act as 'sappers' or combat engineers and opened the way for their unit during marches or on the battlefield. Their main task was that of removing all the obstacles that their comrades could encounter during an operation, especially when the battalion was moving across broken terrain such as that covered by trees or by defensive structures built by the enemy.

In addition to the headquarters, there were the ten companies in a battalion: eight 'centre' companies made up of fusiliers, one 'right flank' company of grenadiers and one 'left flank' company of light infantrymen.

Composition of a company

Each company consisted of one captain, two lieutenants or ensigns, two sergeants, three corporals, one drummer, one fifer and 90 privates.

On paper, each battalion was to deploy 1,000 soldiers, but the effective average strength varied from less than 500 men to a maximum of 800. The eight 'centre' companies were numbered from one to eight and could be assembled into four 'grand divisions' of two companies each. Collectively, they could be divided into 16 sub divisions, known as 'half-companies', or into 32 sections. Each half-company was to have 50 soldiers, while each section had 25 men.

In 1785, following the American Revolution, the British line infantry was reduced to 77 regiments, most of which had just one battalion each. Following the beginning of the wars with Revolutionary France, from 1793, the line infantry was greatly expanded with the formation of many new regiments and with the addition of second battalions to several of the existing units. At its maximum expansion, the British line infantry could deploy a total of 135 regiments.

Organisational history 1800–15 of line infantry

Each regiment was numbered and also had its own specific denomination frequently deriving from the surname of the colonel who had founded it or from the name of the county where it had been created.

1st Royal Regiment of Foot (Royal Scots)

Raised in 1661, it had two battalions from 1686. A 3rd and 4th Battalion were added in 1804. This regiment was one of just a few in the British line infantry to have four battalions.

Above left: Officer of the 68th Regiment of Foot wearing the M1800 shako. (Photo and © Old 68th Society)

Above right: Line infantry officers wearing M1812 shako.

2nd Regiment of Foot (The Queen's Royal [West Surrey])
Raised in 1661, it had two battalions from 1794. During 1796, the two battalions were merged into one.

3rd Regiment of Foot (The Buffs [Royal East Kent])
Raised in 1672, it had two battalions from 1803. The 2nd Battalion was disbanded in 1816.

4th Regiment of Foot (King's Own Royal [Lancaster])
Raised in 1680, it received a 2nd and 3rd Battalion during 1799. The 3rd Battalion was disbanded in 1802, and the 2nd Battalion was raised again in 1804 and disbanded again in 1815.

5th Regiment of Foot (Royal Northumberland Fusiliers)
Raised in 1684, it had a 2nd Battalion during the years 1799–1803 and later during 1804–16.

6th Regiment of Foot (Royal Warwickshire)
Raised in 1673, it had a 2nd Battalion during 1804–15.

7th Regiment of Foot (Royal Fusiliers)
Raised in 1685, it had a 2nd Battalion during 1795–96 and 1804–15.

8th Regiment of Foot (The King's)
Raised in 1685, it had a 2nd Battalion during 1804–15.

9th Regiment of Foot (East Norfolk)
Raised in 1685, it had a 2nd and 3rd Battalion during 1799–1802. The 2nd Battalion was raised again in 1804–15.

10th Regiment of Foot (North Lincolnshire)
Raised in 1685, it had a 2nd Battalion during 1804–16.

11th Regiment of Foot (North Devonshire)
Raised in 1685, it had a 2nd Battalion from 1808.

12th Regiment of Foot (East Suffolk)
Raised in 1685, it had a 2nd Battalion from 1812.

13th Regiment of Foot (1st Somersetshire)
Raised in 1685, it was a single battalion.

Above left: **Officer of the 68th Regiment of Foot wearing M1812 shako. (Photo and © Old 68th Society)**

Above right: **Colour sergeant of the 32nd Regiment of Foot. (Photo and © 32nd Cornwall Regiment of Foot)**

14th Regiment of Foot (Bedfordshire [Buckinghamshire since 1809])
Raised in 1685, it had a 2nd Battalion during 1804–17 and a 3rd Battalion during 1813–16.

15th Regiment of Foot (Yorkshire East Riding)
Raised in 1685, it had a 2nd Battalion during 1799–1802 and during 1804–14.

16th Regiment of Foot (Buckinghamshire [Bedfordshire since 1809])
Raised in 1688, it was a single battalion.

17th Regiment of Foot (Leicestershire)
Raised in 1688, it had a 2nd Battalion during 1799–1802.

18th Regiment of Foot (The Royal Irish)
Raised in 1684, it had a 2nd Battalion during 1803–14.

19th Regiment of Foot (1st Yorkshire North Riding)
Raised in 1689, it always had a single battalion.

20th Regiment of Foot (East Devonshire)
Raised in 1688, it had a 2nd Battalion during 1799–1802.

21st Regiment of Foot (Royal North British Fusiliers)
Raised in 1678, it had a 2nd Battalion during 1804–16.

22nd Regiment of Foot (Cheshire)
Raised in 1688, it had a 2nd Battalion for some months during 1814.

23rd Regiment of Foot (Royal Welch Fusiliers)
Raised in 1689, it had a 2nd Battalion during 1804–14.

24th Regiment of Foot (2nd Warwickshire)
Raised in 1689, it had a 2nd Battalion during 1804–14.

Above left: NCO of the 68th Regiment of Foot. (Photo and © Old 68th Society)

Above right: NCO of the 23rd Regiment of Foot, wearing oilskin protective cover on the shako. (Photo by Carwyn Balch, copyright by 23rd Regiment of Foot, The Royal Welch Fusileers 1809–1815)

25th Regiment of Foot (Sussex [King's Own Scottish Borderers since 1805])
Raised in 1689, it had a 2nd and 3rd Battalion during 1795–96. The 2nd Battalion was raised again in 1804–16.

26th Regiment of Foot (Cameronian)
Raised in 1689, it had a 2nd Battalion during 1804–14.

27th Regiment of Foot (Inniskilling)
Raised in 1689, it had a 2nd Battalion during 1800–02 and 1804–17. A 3rd Battalion existed in the years 1805–16.

28th Regiment of Foot (North Gloucestershire)
Raised in 1694, it had a 2nd Battalion during 1803–14.

29th Regiment of Foot (Worcestershire)
Raised in 1702, it had a 2nd Battalion during 1795–96.

30th Regiment of Foot (Cambridgeshire)
Raised in 1702, it had a 2nd Battalion during 1803–17.

31st Regiment of Foot (Huntingdonshire)
Raised in 1702, it had a 2nd Battalion during 1804–14.

32nd Regiment of Foot (Cornwall)
Raised in 1702, it had a 2nd Battalion during 1804–14.

33rd Regiment of Foot (1st Yorkshire West Riding)
Raised in 1702, it always had a single battalion.

34th Regiment of Foot (Cumberland)
Raised in 1702, it had a 2nd Battalion during 1805–17.

35th Regiment of Foot (Dorsetshire [Sussex since 1805])
Raised in 1702, it had a 2nd Battalion during 1799–1803 and 1805–17.

36th Regiment of Foot (Herefordshire)
Raised in 1702, it had a 2nd Battalion during 1804–14.

37th Regiment of Foot (North Hampshire)
Raised in 1702, it had a 2nd Battalion during 1813–17.

38th Regiment of Foot (1st Staffordshire)
Raised in 1705, it always had a single battalion.

39th Regiment of Foot (East Middlesex [Dorsetshire since 1807])
Raised in 1702, it had a 2nd Battalion during 1803–14.

40th Regiment of Foot (2nd Somersetshire)
Raised in 1717, it had a 2nd Battalion during 1799–1802 and 1804–15.

41st Regiment of Foot (Royal Invalids)
Raised in 1719, it always had a single battalion.

42nd Regiment of Foot (Royal Highland)
Raised in 1739, it had a 2nd Battalion during 1803–14.

NCO of the 44th Regiment of Foot. (Photo and ©
44th East Essex Regiment of Foot)

43rd Regiment of Foot (Monmouthshire)
Raised in 1741, it had a 2nd Battalion during 1804–17.

44th Regiment of Foot (East Essex)
Raised in 1741, it had a 2nd Battalion during 1803–16.

45th Regiment of Foot (1st Nottinghamshire)
Raised in 1741, it had a 2nd Battalion during 1804–14.

46th Regiment of Foot (South Devonshire)
Raised in 1741, it had a 2nd Battalion during 1800–02.

47th Regiment of Foot (Lancashire)
Raised in 1741, it had a 2nd Battalion during 1803–15.

48th Regiment of Foot (Northamptonshire)
Raised in 1741, it had a 2nd Battalion during 1803–14.

49th Regiment of Foot (Hertfordshire)
Raised in 1743, it had a 2nd Battalion during 1813–14.

50th Regiment of Foot (West Kent)
Raised in 1755, it had a 2nd Battalion during 1804–14.

51st Regiment of Foot (2nd Yorkshire West Riding)
Raised in 1755, it always had a single battalion.

52nd Regiment of Foot (Oxfordshire)
Raised in 1755, it had a 2nd Battalion during 1799–1803 and
1804–16.

53rd Regiment of Foot (Shropshire)
Raised in 1755, it had a 2nd Battalion during 1803–17.

54th Regiment of Foot (West Norfolk)
Raised in 1755, it had a 2nd Battalion during 1800–02.

55th Regiment of Foot (Westmoreland)
Raised in 1755, it always had a single battalion.

56th Regiment of Foot (West Essex)
Raised in 1755, it had a 2nd Battalion during 1804–16 and a
3rd Battalion during 1813–14.

57th Regiment of Foot (West Middlesex)
Raised in 1755, it had a 2nd Battalion during 1803–15.

Corporals of the 68th Regiment of Foot.
(Photo and © Old 68th Society)

Above left: **Fusilier of the 33rd Regiment of Foot. (Photo and © His Majesty's 33rd Regiment of Foot)**

Above middle: **Fusiliers of the 33rd Regiment of Foot, wearing protective oilskin covers on their shakos. (Photo and © His Majesty's 33rd Regiment of Foot)**

Above right: **Private from the light infantry company of the 32nd Regiment of Foot. (Photo and © 32nd Cornwall Regiment of Foot)**

58th Regiment of Foot (Rutlandshire)
Raised in 1755, it had a 2nd Battalion during 1803–15.

59th Regiment of Foot (2nd Nottinghamshire)
Raised in 1755, it had a 2nd Battalion during 1804–16.

60th Regiment of Foot (Royal American)
Raised in 1755, it had four battalions until 1797; in that year, a 5th Battalion was added, followed by a 6th in 1799. In 1813, another two battalions were added, for a total of eight. During 1816–19, the regiment was gradually reduced to just two battalions.

61st Regiment of Foot (South Gloucestershire)
Raised in 1756, it had a 2nd Battalion during 1803–14.

62nd Regiment of Foot (Wiltshire)
Raised in 1756, it had a 2nd Battalion during 1799–1802 and 1804–16.

63rd Regiment of Foot (West Suffolk)
Raised in 1756, it had a 2nd Battalion during 1804–14.

64th Regiment of Foot (2nd Staffordshire)
Raised in 1756, it always had a single battalion.

65th Regiment of Foot (2nd Yorkshire North Riding)
Raised in 1756, it always had a single battalion.

66th Regiment of Foot (Berkshire)
Raised in 1756, it had a 2nd Battalion during 1803–17.

67th Regiment of Foot (South Hampshire)
Raised in 1756, it had a 2nd Battalion during 1803–17.

68th Regiment of Foot (Durham)
Raised in 1755, it had a 2nd Battalion during 1800–02.

69th Regiment of Foot (South Lincolnshire)
Raised in 1758, it had a 2nd Battalion during 1794–95 and 1803–16.

70th Regiment of Foot (Surrey [Glasgow Lowland since 1812])
Raised in 1758, it always had a single battalion.

71st Regiment of Foot (Glasgow Highland)
Raised in 1777, it had a 2nd Battalion during 1804–15.

72nd Regiment of Foot (Seaforth's Highlanders)
Raised in 1777, it had a 2nd Battalion during 1804–16.

73rd Regiment of Foot
Raised in 1786, it had a 2nd Battalion during 1808–17.

74th Regiment of Foot
Raised in 1787, it always had a single battalion.

75th Regiment of Foot
Raised in 1787, it always had a single battalion.

76th Regiment of Foot
Raised in 1787, it always had a single battalion.

77th Regiment of Foot (East Middlesex)
Raised in 1787, it always had a single battalion.

78th Regiment of Foot (Ross-Shire Buffs)
Raised in 1793, it had a 2nd Battalion during 1794–96 and 1804–16.

Private of the 51st Regiment of Foot; the unit was transformed into a light infantry regiment during 1809. (ASKB)

79th Regiment of Foot (Cameron Highlanders)
Raised in 1793, it had a 2nd Battalion during 1805–15.

80th Regiment of Foot (Staffordshire Volunteers)
Raised in 1793, it always had a single battalion.

81st Regiment of Foot (Loyal Lincoln Volunteers)
Raised in 1793, it had a 2nd Battalion during 1803–16.

82nd Regiment of Foot (Prince of Wales' Volunteers)
Raised in 1793, it had a 2nd Battalion during 1804–15.

83rd Regiment of Foot (County of Dublin)
Raised in 1793, it had a 2nd Battalion during 1804–17.

84th Regiment of Foot (York and Lancaster)
Raised in 1793, it had a 2nd Battalion during 1794–95 and 1808–19.

85th Regiment of Foot (Bucks Volunteers)
Raised in 1793, it had a 2nd Battalion during 1800–02.

86th Regiment of Foot (Shropshire Volunteers [Leinster since 1806])
Raised in 1793, it had a 2nd Battalion during 1813–14.

87th Regiment of Foot (Prince of Wales' Irish)
Raised in 1793, it had a 2nd Battalion during 1804–17.

88th Regiment of Foot (Connaught Rangers)
Raised in 1793, it had a 2nd Battalion during 1804–16.

89th Regiment of Foot
Raised in 1793, it had a 2nd Battalion during 1804–16.

90th Regiment of Foot (Perthshire Volunteers)
Raised in 1793, it had a 2nd Battalion during 1794–96 and 1804–16.

Among the various regiments listed above, there were several light infantry and Scots regiments. These 90 regiments could be divided into nine groups according to their date of origin:

- Regiments 1–6 were raised following the Restoration of Charles II (1660) to the English throne.
- Regiments 7–15 were created during the reorganisation of the English Army by James II (1633–1701), around 1685.
- Regiments 16–28 (excluding regiments 18, 21 and 28) were formed after the Glorious Revolution (1688) of William of Orange (1650–1702).
- Regiments 29–41 were organised during the mobilisation for the War of the Spanish Succession (1701–15).

Above left: Corporal of the 68th Regiment of Foot; the regiment was transformed into a light infantry regiment during 1808. (Photo and © Old 68th Society)

Above right: Private of the 32nd Regiment of Foot wearing winter greatcoat. (Photo and © 32nd Cornwall Regiment of Foot)

- Regiments 42–49 were raised during the mobilisation for the War of the Austrian Succession (1740–1748).
- Regiments 50–70 were created due to the outbreak of the Seven Years' War (1756–63).
- Regiments 71–72 were organised due to the outbreak of the American Revolution (1775–83).
- Regiments 73–77 were formed for service in India.
- Regiments 78–90 were raised soon after the outbreak of hostilities with Revolutionary France (1778)

The seven infantry regiments organised during the 1780s were all employed during the Third Anglo-Mysore War (1790–92), one of the greatest conflicts fought by Britain in India. Since the war was being carried on by the British East India Company and not by the British Crown, it was the commercial enterprise that paid for the expenses deriving from the formation of these regiments (according to the Declaratory Act of 1788). When many European countries formed a military coalition to limit the territorial ambitions of Revolutionary France, Britain had no choice but to expand its military forces in view of the new campaigns to be fought. This led to the creation of 13 new infantry regiments, most of which were originally raised as volunteer units and later transformed into line corps. The patriotic response to the outbreak of a new war was incredible and made it possible to enlarge the numbers of foot troops substantially.

During the period 1793–96, another 45 infantry regiments (numbered 91–135) were recruited, all having a single battalion. These had a very ephemeral history and had all been disbanded by the beginning of 1797. As a result, their progressive numbers were later given to new units, which had a much longer life. The following new regiments (numbered 91–104) were created during the period 1794–1815 and had a stable history:

91st Regiment of Foot (Argyllshire Highlanders)
Raised in 1794, it had a 2nd Battalion during 1804–15.

92nd Regiment of Foot (Gordon Highlanders)
Raised in 1794, it had a 2nd Battalion during 1803–14.

Above left: Drum major (left) and 'sapper' (a soldier acting as a combat engineer) of the line infantry.

Above right: Sapper of the 68th Regiment of Foot. (Photo and © Old 68th Society)

93rd Regiment of Foot (Sutherland Highlanders)
Raised in 1799, it had a 2nd Battalion during 1813–15.

94th Regiment of Foot (Scotch Brigade)
Raised in 1794, but only receiving its number in 1802. It always had a single battalion.

95th Regiment of Foot (Rifles)
Raised in 1800, it had a 2nd Battalion from 1805 and a 3rd Battalion from 1809. The 3rd Battalion was disbanded in 1819.

96th Regiment of Foot
Raised in 1803, it had a 2nd Battalion since 1804.

97th Regiment of Foot (Queen's Own Germans)
Raised in 1798, it always had a single battalion.

98th Regiment of Foot
Raised in 1804, it always had a single battalion.

99th Regiment of Foot (Prince of Wales' Tipperary Regiment)
Raised in 1804, it always had a single battalion.

100th Regiment of Foot (Prince Regent's County of Dublin)
Raised in 1804, it always had a single battalion.

101st Regiment of Foot (Duke of York's Irish)
Raised in 1805, it always had a single battalion.

102nd Regiment of Foot
Raised in 1789 as the 'New South Wales Corps', it became a line regiment in 1808.

103rd Regiment of Foot
Raised in 1806 as a 'Royal Veteran Battalion', it became a line regiment in 1808.

104th Regiment of Foot
Raised in 1803 as the 'New Brunswick Fencibles', it became a line regiment in 1810.

Among the regiments listed above, the 94th had an interesting history. This was a Scottish unit commanded by officers who had previously served as part of the Dutch Army's 'Scots Brigade'. Since the Eighty Years' War, also known as the Dutch Revolt (1568–1648), which secured the independence of the Netherlands from Spain, the Dutch Army had comprised a mixed Anglo-Scottish Brigade with three English regiments and three Scottish ones. During the Glorious Revolution (1688) the Anglo-Scottish regiments of William of Orange followed him during his conquest of the English throne. Following these events, the three English regiments became part of William's reformed English Army while the three Scottish ones went back to the Netherlands (assuming the denomination of Scots Brigade). The Scots Brigade took part in all the wars fought by the Dutch Army during the 18th century, until 1782 when the ongoing Fourth Anglo-Dutch War (1780–84) caused great malcontent among the Scots and forced the Dutch

Above left: Drummer of the 5th Regiment of Foot. (ASKB)

Above right: Drummer boy of the 33rd Regiment of Foot. (Photo and © His Majesty's 33rd Regiment of Foot)

to transform the three regiments into Dutch ones. Most of the Scottish soldiers abandoned the Netherlands and joined the British Army, while several of their officers asked the British government to create a new Scots Brigade that would have been part of the British Army. Their request was not accepted until the outbreak of war with Revolutionary France, when 23 of them were permitted to raise the new 94th Regiment of Foot that would have been known as Scotch Brigade.

The 97th Regiment was recruited in Menorca from German-speaking prisoners of war coming from the Swiss regiments of the Spanish Army. During 1796–1808, Spain was an ally of Revolutionary France and thus at war with Britain. At that time, the Spanish Army comprised six mercenary infantry regiments made up of Swiss soldiers, from which the recruits of the 97th Regiment came.

The last three regiments, numbered 102–104, were originally raised as different kinds of infantry units; their history is reviewed in the following chapters.

Considering the population of Britain (9 million in 1801), a general infantry establishment of more than 100 regiments was impressive for the standards of the Napoleonic Wars. In addition, these regiments were of high quality. Of all the 104 line infantry regiments listed in this chapter, ten were Irish units:

- 18th Regiment of Foot (Royal Irish)
- 27th Regiment of Foot (Inniskilling)
- 83rd Regiment of Foot (County of Dublin)
- 86th Regiment of Foot (Shropshire Volunteers)
- 87th Regiment of Foot (Prince of Wales' Irish)
- 88th Regiment of Foot (Connaught Rangers)
- 89th Regiment of Foot
- 99th Regiment of Foot (Prince of Wales' Tipperary Regiment)
- 100th Regiment of Foot (Prince Regent's County of Dublin), and
- 101st Regiment of Foot (Duke of York's Irish)

Of these, some had a very remarkable history, including the Royal Irish and the Inniskilling.

The Royal Irish was raised in 1684 by assembling independent garrison companies that existed in Ireland. During the Glorious Revolution, it supported William of Orange and so was not disbanded like all the other Irish units. As a result, it was the oldest of the Irish regiments serving in the British Army. The Inniskilling was raised in 1689 as a local militia unit, recruited from those Irishmen who supported William of Orange during his struggle against James II. The unit fought with great courage during the Williamite War in Ireland (1689–91) and in 1690, it was made part of the English Army.

Chapter 3

The Highland Infantry

The Scottish regiments were a fundamental component of the British infantry even before the creation of Great Britain. In fact, five important units of the English Army were recruited from Scotland before 1707:

- 3rd Foot Guards
- 1st Regiment of Foot
- 21st Regiment of Foot
- 25th Regiment of Foot
- 26th Regiment of Foot

All these corps, however, were recruited from the Scottish Lowlands and not from the Highlands. They wore the same uniforms as the English line infantrymen so that their members were practically undistinguishable from each other. The Lowlands had always been strongly linked with England and had accepted English rule. The Highlands, however, had always guarded their Scottish freedom and did not accept union with England for long time. The Highlanders were, without doubt, the best fighters of the British Isles, and rose up against the English several times during the 18th century, preventing the military from raising regular units from the population. This situation started to change after the crushing of the Jacobite rising of 1745, the last great rebellion of the Highlanders. In time, in fact, it was possible to form several regiments of Highlanders that soon became an elite inside the British Army. Wearing traditional uniforms and with their own denominations, these regiments differed from the other Scottish units raised from the Lowlands.

By 1802, the following Scottish regiments were part of the British infantry:

- 3rd Foot Guards [Lowlanders]
- 1st Foot Regiment (Royal Scots) [Lowlanders]
- 21st Foot Regiment (Royal North British Fusiliers) [Lowlanders]
- 25th Foot Regiment (King's Own Scottish Borderers) [Lowlanders]
- 26th Foot Regiment (Cameronian) [Lowlanders]
- 42nd Foot Regiment (Royal Highland) [Highlanders]
- 70th Foot Regiment (Glasgow Lowland) [Lowlanders]
- 71st Foot Regiment (Glasgow Highland) [Highlanders]
- 72nd Foot Regiment (Seaforth's Highlanders) [Highlanders]
- 73rd Foot Regiment [Highlanders]
- 74th Foot Regiment [Highlanders]
- 75th Foot Regiment [Highlanders]
- 78th Foot Regiment (Ross-Shire Buffs) [Highlanders]
- 79th Foot Regiment (Cameron Highlanders) [Highlanders]
- 91st Foot Regiment (Argyllshire Highlanders) [Highlanders]
- 92nd Foot Regiment (Gordon Highlanders) [Highlanders]
- 93rd Foot Regiment (Sutherland Highlanders) [Highlanders]
- 94th Foot Regiment (Scotch Brigade) [Lowlanders]

Above left: Officer of the Gordon Highlanders wearing the jacket with the frontal lapels buttoned up. (Photo and © Gordon's Living History)

Above middle: Officer of the Cameron Highlanders.

Above right: Officer of the Gordon Highlanders wearing the jacket with the frontal lapels unbuttoned. (Photo and © Gordon's Living History)

A total of 18 line infantry regiments were recruited in Scotland, of which seven came from the Lowlands and 11 from the Highlands. The Lowlander's units had the same history as their English equivalents (except for the 94th Regiment, as noted above), while each of the Highlanders had their own history. After the Jacobite rising of 1715, the British Army did not have enough resources to leave a strong garrison force in the Highlands to control the territory. As a result, it was forced to keep order among the Highlanders by recruiting men from local clans loyal to the British Crown. These new soldiers would have been employed mostly as rural policemen, to counter cattle rustling and the other regular crimes typical in the Highlands in the 18th century.

In 1725, the first units of loyal Highlanders were raised, and known as the Independent Highland Companies. The officers of these corps were commissioned by the British Army, while their men had a semi-regular status and could not be considered 'proper' soldiers. Independent Highland Companies had already existed during the 17th century and been disbanded in 1717. By re-forming them, the British government hoped to maintain peace in the northern regions of Scotland. Initially only three companies, with little more than 100 men each, were raised. Later, another three companies with more or less 70 men in each were organised. The companies were recruited from the members of Clan Munro, another from Clan Fraser of Lovat. Clan Grant members filled another company and the remainder of the six companies were all recruited from Clan Campbell. Collectively, they were known as the Black Watch, because of the dark colour of the tartan from which their kilts were made.

In 1739, another four companies were added to the corps, bringing the total to ten. During that same year, they were assembled to form the 42nd Regiment of Foot of the line infantry, which was the first Highland regular unit to enter British service). When the second Jacobite rising broke out, the regiment was fighting in Europe as part of Britain's participation in the War of Austrian Succession (1740–48). As a result, three additional companies were formed for service in Scotland and fought against the Jacobites until they were disbanded in 1748. Meanwhile, to suppress the Jacobite rising, the British government had ordered the raising of 18 new Independent Highland Companies to replace those that had been transformed into the 42nd Regiment. Once the rising was crushed, the new companies were disbanded permanently. During the following decades, the 42nd Foot Regiment (Black Watch) took part in all the most important military campaigns fought by the British Army including the Seven Years' War and the American Revolutionary War.

Highland infantry at war

- During the Napoleonic Wars, the **1st Battalion of the 42nd Foot Regiment** took part in Egypt in 1801, Iberian Peninsula in 1808, Walcheren in 1809, Iberian Peninsula in 1812–14 and Waterloo in 1815.
- The **2nd Battalion of the 42nd Foot Regiment**, instead, fought in the Peninsula during 1810–12.
- The **1st Battalion of the 71st Foot Regiment** participated in the following campaigns: Cape of Good Hope (South Africa) (1806) and La Plata (Argentina) (1806), Peninsula (1808), Walcheren (1809), Peninsula (1810–14) and Waterloo (1815).
- The **2nd Battalion of the 71st Foot Regiment** remained as a garrison in Britain.
- The **1st Battalion of the 72nd Foot Regiment** remained as a garrison in South Africa for most of the Napoleonic period
- The **2nd Battalion of the 72nd Foot Regiment** did not leave Ireland during the period taken into account.
- The **1st Battalion of the 73rd Foot Regiment** garrisoned New South Wales from 1809.
- The **2nd Battalion of the 73rd Foot Regiment** fought in the Netherlands (1814) and at Waterloo (1815).
- The **74th Foot Regiment** served at Walcheren (1809) and later in the Peninsular War (1811–14).
- The **75th Foot Regiment** was stationed in Sicily during the years 1811–14.
- The **1st Battalion of the 78th Foot Regiment** took part in the British occupation of Java during 1811–16, while the **2nd Battalion** fought in Sicily (1806) and at Walcheren (1809) before participating to the Belgian Campaign of 1815.
- The **79th Foot Regiment** took part in the Egyptian Campaign of 1801 and in the Danish one of 1807, before fighting in the Peninsula (1810–14) and at Waterloo (1815).

- The **1st Battalion of the 91st Foot Regiment** was sent to Walcheren in 1809 and later to the Peninsula (1812–14). It later took part in the Belgian Campaign of 1815. **The 2nd Battalion**, instead, was in the Netherlands during the campaign of 1814.
- The **1st Battalion of the 92nd Foot Regiment** participated in the Egyptian Campaign in 1801 and in the Danish one of 1807. Later it was sent to Walcheren (1809) and to the Peninsula (1810–14) before fighting at Waterloo. The 2nd Battalion of the same unit remained in Ireland.
- The **93rd Foot Regiment** was stationed in South Africa until 1814, before being sent to North America in 1815 to fight at New Orleans.

Generally, the Highlanders were excellent soldiers. They could be less disciplined than their English equivalents, but their courage and fitness were unrivalled. They could defend a position to the last man and were extremely proud of their regimental traditions. On many occasions, they were able to achieve success despite numerical inferiority, and their morale was usually very high. The Highlanders were used to living in a poor and rocky countryside, where conditions of life were extremely harsh. As a result, they could endure hardships of any kind while on campaign and could live for days with

Above left: **Private of the Seaforth's Highlanders.**

Above middle: **Private of the Cameron Highlanders. (Photo and © The 79th Cameron Highlanders)**

Above right: **NCO of the Gordon Highlanders from the light company of the regiment. (Photo and © Gordon's Living History)**

very little food. These mountaineers were able to move very rapidly on every kind of terrain and thus had excellent skirmishing abilities. In combat, the Highlanders were prone to using their bayonets much more frequently than their English equivalents, since their fighting spirit was still that of the ancient Celtic warriors. When needed, however, they could deliver a very accurate fire upon the enemy ranks. From an organisational point of view, the Scottish regiments had exactly the same structure as the English ones; their musicians, however, played bagpipes instead of fifes.

Right: Bagpiper of the Glasgow Highlanders. (ASKB)

Below left and below middle: Private of the Gordon Highlanders from the light company of the regiment. (Photo and © Gordon's Living History)

Below right: Sapper of the Cameron Highlanders. (Photo and © The 79th Cameron Highlanders)

Chapter 4

The Light Infantry

D uring the first seven decades of the 18th century, the line infantry was the most important component of the European armies, since it made up the bulk of the troops mobilised and also because it had acquired a tactical superiority over the cavalry. Highly trained and well disciplined, it consisted of fusiliers who were able to march and manoeuvre in perfect order by maintaining 'shoulder-to-shoulder' close formations. While moving on the battlefield, the line infantrymen advanced in columns. When stopping to open fire upon the enemy, they were deployed into long lines. After some rolling volleys of musketry were exchanged between the two opposing infantry formations, a clash could continue in two different ways. On most occasions, one of the two lines was shattered by the enemy fire and retreated (usually keeping order among the ranks and re-adopting column formation). On some occasions, instead, it was necessary to fight 'hand-to-hand' with bayonets. Keeping order in the formations and delivering a regular fire were the key factors behind victory; as a result, training was absolutely decisive to transform line infantry into an effective tactical tool.

Battle tactics

Generally, battles were extremely static, since maintaining perfect order in the formations obliged the infantrymen to move very slowly. The transition from the column formation to the line formation was extremely delicate, since it exposed the fusiliers to the sudden charges of cavalry. When confronting

Officer of the 95th Rifles (left), private of the 95th Rifles (centre) and private of the 5th Battalion/60th Foot (right).

the cavalry, line infantry usually adopted a standard defensive formation known as 'square': this was another kind of close order, created with the aim of stopping enemy attacks by using the bayonets as pikes against mounted troops. The formations and tactics described were determined by the performance of the muskets that were used during the 18th century. Muskets were flintlock weapons, with complicated loading operations. This meant that only one or two balls were shot in a minute by a line infantryman with good training. In addition, the flintlock muskets of this period were all smoothbores and were extremely inaccurate. When a ball was fired, it came out from the weapon without a precise direction since there were no grooves inside the barrel to guide it. A flintlock musket was of service when fired at 100 or 200 metres from the target. As a result, during a battle, the line infantry formations had to come very close to the enemy in order to use their weapons with some degree of effectiveness. The muskets of this age were also extremely heavy and this limited the mobility of the foot soldiers. When moving over diverse terrain covered with rocks or trees, it was practically impossible for them to keep the close formations in order. All the main tactical formations had been created for an 'ideal' battlefield, consisting of a large plain where the opposing infantries could move without encountering obstacles. In this military system, soldiers were not required to think and act in an autonomous way. They only had to move as directed by their training to put into practice the orders received. There was no space for initiative and each infraction of discipline was immediately punished with very harsh methods. The manoeuvres required on the battlefield were repeated every day during training sessions, under the incessant beat of drums.

A perfect example of the kind of war that was fought in the 18th century was represented by the Prussian Army of Frederick the Great (1712–1786). He perfected close infantry tactics and was admired by all the officer corps of Europe. His infantrymen were the best in the world and their methods of training were copied by all armies whether enemies or allies. During the War of Austrian Succession and the Seven Years' War, however, some battles revealed that the Prussian line infantry was imperfect. It became apparent that it could experience serious problems while operating on broken terrain and when fighting enemy units that employed 'hit-and-run' guerrilla tactics. In particular, the Prussians had serious problems countering the efficient light troops deployed by the Austrian Empire: these consisted of semi-regular light infantrymen, recruited from the inhabitants of the Balkans.

Open formation tactics

The light infantrymen of the Austrian Army had been fighting for decades against the Ottoman Turks on the southern frontier of the Austrian Empire. It was a time of endless conflict, during which both sides launched rapid incursions into the territory of the enemy to raid and pillage as much as possible. Gradually, the Austrian frontier soldiers learned to fight like their enemies, becoming expert at skirmishing and scouting. Their usual area of operations was covered by mountains and woods, where each soldier had to move singularly and not in a column or line formation. Most of these soldiers were excellent huntsmen in their civilian lives and were also farmers, living on the Balkan frontier as military settlers. As a result, their innovative tactics derived from hunting were based on the principle of open formation. Each soldier was to advance in an autonomous way, but keep in contact with the other members of his unit; this way he could cover his advance behind the obstacles of the terrain (such as a tree, for example) and fire upon the enemy from a favourable position. On several occasions, the Austrian light infantrymen caused serious trouble and losses to Frederick the Great's perfect line infantry. Initially, they were considered dishonourable killers by traditionalist enemies, but during the course of the Seven Years' War, it became apparent that their tactics could play a very important role on the battlefields. The other great powers of Europe, unlike Austria, could not count on a militarised border from which expert light fighters could be recruited. As a result, they started to create their own light infantry corps from the best hunters and gamekeepers of their communities. New units soon assumed the denomination of chasseurs or 'jagers' (hunters). The members of these corps were usually dressed in green like most contemporary civilian hunters and communicated with horns and not with drums. During the Seven Years' War, dozens of new light corps were raised in France and Prussia, following the Austrian example. These proved their efficiency on campaign, and a new branch of the infantry was effectively born.

Skirmishers

The conflict of 1756–63 was fought in the Americas, where there was a terrible clash between the British and French colonies located in the northern part of the New World. In North America, however, the tactical ability of the armies was completely different from that of Europe and where some form of local

**Officers of the 1st Battalion/95th Rifles. (Photo and ©
1/95th Rifles Living History Society)**

light infantry had existed for a century. The terrain of the Thirteen British Colonies, as well as that of French Canada (New France), was mostly covered with dense forests and was inhabited by native communities whose warriors fought as lightly armed and highly mobile skirmishers. Colonial warfare consisted of rapid raids and incursions launched across the frontier, exactly like the southern border of the Austrian Empire. As a result, British and French colonists/farmers were also militiamen with great skirmishing capabilities. In order to survive, each settler had to learn hunting in the forests and fighting the natives using these same methods. In 1675, the first great war in the history of Colonial America was fought between the English colonists and the native Indian tribes. This conflict is commonly known as King Philip's War (1675–76), from the nickname that the colonists gave to their main native opponent (his true name was Metacomet [1638–1676]). The war consisted of a great native insurgency that took place on the borders of the English colonies, which could potentially lead to the expulsion of the whites from that part of North America. By using their hit-and-run guerrilla tactics, the native warriors of Metacomet caused many losses to the colonial militia and destroyed an impressive number of English settlements. Following that experience, however, the colonial authorities created a light infantry corps that could oppose the native attacks by using the same tactics. Command of this new experimental unit was given to Benjamin Church (c. 1639–1718), a settler with combat experience in similar terrain. The members of the new corps, consisting of a single company, were known as rangers. During the second half of the conflict, Church's men obtained a series of important victories over the native peoples and killed Metacomet during a skirmish in the woods. The inclusion of light infantry was a key factor in the final victory of the colonists.

Light infantry in North America – the Royal American

From 1675, all the colonies of North America started to have their own chosen units of rangers, which were deployed on the frontier with native territories: light infantry was born in the New World. What had been achieved in North America, however, was not learned in Europe. No English troops had participated in King Philip's War and thus Benjamin Church's innovations did not reach Europe. At that time, the American colonies were considered as a secondary 'theatre of operations', and this did not change until the outbreak of the French-Indian War (which commenced in 1754, two years before the Seven Years' War in Europe). During that conflict, the British Army had to intervene in the Thirteen Colonies with substantial contingents of troops in order to counter the expansionist ambitions of the French. In controlling Canada, the French had formed important political alliances with most of the native tribes and were in control of the fur trade of North America. French colonists were all potential light infantrymen, since they were not farmers (as the British) but hunters who lived in close contact with native tribes. After the raids launched by the French militia in tandem with native allies caused a series of massacres among the British settlers, it became apparent that the ranger units in North America had to be expanded and augmented with the creation of new light corps. As a result, several ranger units were organised; these, however, these remained provincial and for service in the Americas only. They were not included into the official establishment of the British Army.

In 1756, however, it was finally decided to create the first regular light infantry unit of the British Army. This step was taken as the result of a disastrous defeat suffered by the British line infantry in 1754 at the Battle of Monongahela. The defeat saw the ambush of 1,300 British soldiers by a smaller force of French and native allies, who annihilated their opponents. The British contingent included line infantrymen from the 44th and 48th Foot, in addition to provincial soldiers of the Virginia Regiment commanded by the young George Washington. The British lost more than 450 men during the ambush and were unable to counter the enemy's skirmishing tactics in an effective way.

The new light infantry unit created after the Battle of Monongahela was initially known as the 62nd Regiment of Foot (Royal American), since it adopted its definitive progressive number (60th) only at a later date. Approval for the raising of this new regiment, as well as the necessary funds were granted by the British Parliament in the last days of 1755. The new unit would have comprised four battalions with 1,000 soldiers in each and its main function would have been that of countering raids launched by the French and by their native allies against the settlements of the Thirteen Colonies. The regiment would have been recruited from colonists who already had experience of light infantry tactics as well as from foreigners who had hunting capabilities.

The British Army was specifically interested in recruiting German hunters and gamekeepers like those who were already serving in the light corps of the Prussian and French armies. To count on such experienced personnel, in 1756, the Parliament passed the *Commissions to Foreign Protestants Act* that permitted the recruiting of foreign officers coming from German states and Swiss cantons. These could be employed in the new 62nd Foot, but could not rise above the rank of lieutenant-colonel. In total, about 50 officers of the regiment came from Germany or Switzerland.

Overall command of the unit was given to General John Campbell (at that time commander-in-chief of the British Army in North America).

NCO of the 1st Battalion/95th Rifles. (Photo and © 1/95th Rifles Living History Society)

The original idea behind the formation of the new unit had been of Jacques Prevost (1736–1781), a Swiss soldier and adventurer who was a personal friend of the Duke of Cumberland (1721–1765) second son of King George II (1683 –1760). Prevost was an expert in forest warfare and one of the first to understand the combat potential of light infantry. In general terms, the Royal American Regiment would have united the main features of a provincial (colonial) corps with those of a foreign (mercenary) one. It would have merged the light infantry traditions of North America (rangers) with those of Central Europe (jagers). All members of the unit were Protestants, which was a calculated choice as their direct opponents were French Catholics.

Quite curiously, the Royal American Regiment was the first British unit to have foreign officers but did not comprise any officer from the American colonies. In February 1757, the unit became the 60th Foot, after two line regiments were disbanded. The foreign officers of the regiment included two notable personalities, Henri Bouquet ([1719–1765] who commanded the 1st Battalion) and Frederick Haldimand ([1718–1791] who commanded the 2nd Battalion). Both these Swiss professionals were great contributors to the development of light infantry doctrines inside the British Army. Their progressive ideas included the introduction (unofficial, for the moment) of rifled muskets among the ranks. These new weapons, which had extremely long barrels and spiral grooves in the bore, were produced on a small scale during the early 18th century. They had become popular in the American colonies because of the German gunsmiths who immigrated to the New World and brought these new muskets with them. Because of their superior degree of precision, these rifles were the ideal weapon for hunting and fighting in the woods of North America; and over time were gradually adopted as personal weapons by all the colonists/militiamen of the Thirteen Colonies.

This superior flintlock musket was not adopted by armies in Europe for a long time and continued to be used only for hunting. During the Seven Years' War, some of the newly formed light corps of the European armies started to adopt rifle carbines, at the same time as soldiers from the Royal American Regiment began substituting their smoothbores with rifle muskets. The production costs of these new weapons were high, but using such a weapon could determine the outcome of a battle due to its high level of accuracy. The French-Indian War (1754–63) was the first conflict during which rifles were used on a quite large scale; it would take another 80 years, however, to see the adoption of rifle muskets in the line infantry (it happened in most European armies around 1840).

Bouquet and Haldimand also modified the standard uniforms of the British line infantry to make them more comfortable. The long coat tails were shortened to improve mobility and the coloured lapels were buttoned up to be more practical.

During the French-Indian War, the 60th Foot fought with enormous courage during several of the most important engagements, earning a solid reputation and the famous motto 'Celer et Audax' (Swift and Bold). To keep its soldiers in the ranks of the British armed forces, the British parliament passed the *American Protestant Soldier Naturalization Act*, which offered naturalisation to all foreign officers and soldiers who had served under the Union Jack for at least two years.

Armed with rifled muskets and hatchets, the forest fighters of the Royal American Regiment participated in Pontiac's War (1763). This was a large colonial conflict. The natives, who had been allied to the French, did not accept British victory in the Seven Years' War and rebelled against the British crown, following the expulsion of the French from North America. Some years later, during the American Revolutionary War, the 3rd and 4th Battalions of the 60th Foot were returned to their full complement of infantry, after having been reduced for some years. New soldiers were recruited from Britain and Hanover.

During the period 1714–1837, Hanover was an independent German state whose head of state was the King of Great Britain. Hanover delivered a good number of expert German hunters and gamekeepers to the 60th Foot who fought with distinction during the American Revolution and remained loyal to the Crown despite comprising large numbers of American privates. During the war, it was an example to follow for many of the new provincial units of loyalists that were raised in North America to support the British Army. Many of these new corps were light infantry or light cavalry, equipped with rifled weapons; they performed auxiliary duties for the British, since they were made up of colonists who had great experience of fighting in the forests (most of them were veterans of the provincial units raised during the French-Indian War). After the end of the American Revolutionary War, however, all the loyalist corps were disbanded.

The 60th Regiment of Foot continued to serve in the British Army and remained its only light unit for several years. A 5th Battalion was raised in 1797 by using the soldiers of a German mercenary regiment (Hompesch's Mounted Riflemen) that had been recently disbanded. A 6th Battalion was added in 1799, being formed with German recruits. Finally, another two battalions were raised during 1813 for service in the Americas during the War of 1812 against the United States. These last two battalions were recruited from German and Swiss prisoners of war who had been part of Napoleon's military forces. The 60th Regiment of Foot continued to be strongly linked to the Americas during the Napoleonic Wars and remained the British foot regiment with the highest percentage of German/Swiss personnel.

Of the eight battalions, only the fifth, raised in 1797, was entirely armed with rifles; the original four battalions, in fact, had just one company equipped with rifled carbines. The 6th Battalion, organised in 1799, also had one company armed with rifles, while the last two battalions, formed in 1813, had two rifle companies each.

From 1797, rifle units in the British light infantry started to dress in dark green so that the entire 5th Battalion wore green. The remaining companies, armed with smoothbores, continued to wear standard red uniforms.

The 60th Regiment of Foot at War

- The 1st Battalion was in Canada until 1798. It later transferred to the West Indies (Jamaica) before being sent to South Africa in 1811.
- The 2nd Battalion remained in Canada until 1800, then transferred to the West Indies where it remained for the entire Napoleonic Wars.
- The 3rd Battalion was in the West Indies during 1793–1815.
- The 4th Battalion remained in the Caribbean except

Private of the 1st Battalion/95th Rifles. (Photo and © 1/95th Rifles Living History Society)

for a brief period during 1806–08 when it was sent in South Africa.
- The 5th Battalion served in Ireland until 1799, when it absorbed the soldiers of the recently disbanded German mercenary regiment Löwenstein's Chasseurs. From 1800 to 1806, the battalion served the Americas, before being sent to the Iberian Peninsula where it fought during 1808–14.
- The 6th Battalion was always stationed in Jamaica.
- The 7th Battalion existed only for a few years and always remained in Canada.
- The 8th Battalion had a very short lifespan, spent in Gibraltar as a garrison unit.

Minutemen

During the American Revolution, the British Army had to face the famed Minutemen: these were the militiamen of the Thirteen Colonies, who were able to assemble their companies and be ready to fight in just one minute, if needed. These irregular fighters were all armed with rifled muskets (Kentucky rifles), and were skilled skirmishers, excellent marksmen and knew how to conceal themselves in the woods. They caused serious trouble for the British line infantry, especially during the first phase of the conflict. Minutemen avoided fighting in the open field and were able to move much more rapidly than their British opponents.

In 1758, each British line battalion had been ordered to train one of its companies as light infantry, but this measure was abolished with the end of the Seven Years' War. In 1771, a single light company was re-introduced in all the line battalions, but this measure had not yet been fully implemented when the conflict in the Thirteen Colonies began. As a result, to counter the Minutemen, the British had to rely almost entirely on its ranger and light corps organised by American loyalists. In addition, the British Army could also employ its Highland regiments as light infantry units, since the Scottish mountaineers frequently had all the characteristics of excellent light infantrymen despite being linesmen.

Urgent reforms in the British Army

With the end of the bloody American conflict, all the loyalist light corps were disbanded, together with the temporary battalions that had been formed by assembling light companies from different regiments. The British infantry was greatly reduced in number, but the lessons learned about light infantry fighting were not completely forgotten; one light company was retained in all the battalions. The British light infantry still had many limits. Its soldiers were armed with flintlock smoothbores. Secondly, the prejudices of traditional officers towards light infantry were strong. As a result of this situation, during the Revolutionary Wars with France, the British Army had to rely on recruiting foreign/mercenary regiments from continental Europe in order to have enough light infantrymen.

It is important to remember that the light infantry units were usually short-lived and were never considered a significant component of the British military forces. This situation changed only with the progression of the Revolutionary Wars, during which the French light infantry showed its mastery on several occasions. The British superior officers finally realised that reform was urgently needed, if their army was to face French chasseurs on almost equal terms. The first step towards this was taken in 1798, when the Duke of York authorised the publication of the *Regulations for the Exercise of Riflemen and Light Infantry*. It was written by the commander of the 60th Foot's 5th Battalion and was the first manual for light infantry in the British Army. Its publication marked the beginning of an important debate that took place inside the officer corps. The most traditionalist officers did not want to create new independent regiments of light infantry and still considered the formation of temporary light battalions as the best way to have light corps when needed. Other, more innovative, officers wanted to select the fittest and most intelligent officers/rankers from all the existing line regiments to create new light infantry units. Innovation prevailed. The victories of Revolutionary France had isolated Great Britain from the rest of Europe and had made the recruiting of mercenary light infantrymen coming from the continent virtually impossible.

In January 1800, each of the following line regiments was required to send one captain, one lieutenant, one ensign, two sergeants, one corporal and 30 of its best privates to be trained as riflemen: 1st Foot (2nd Battalion), 21st, 23rd, 25th, 27th, 29th, 49th, 69th, 71st, 72nd, 79th, 85th and 92nd Foot. The chosen men, the best marksmen of their units, would make up a new independent corps of riflemen. Of the selected regiments, half were Scottish, since these already had a light infantry status and were famed for the hardiness of their men. The initial idea of the Duke of York was to train these elite soldiers as riflemen then return them to their original units in order to act as the core for the formation of rifle companies in each line regiment.

Riflemen

The temporary training unit that had just been created received the denomination of Experimental Corps of Riflemen and was commanded by Colonel Coote Manningham (1765–1809) an expert light infantry officer of the British Army. Manningham trained the riflemen according to his own innovative ideas, which were published in 1800 as the *Regulations for the Rifle Corps formed at Blachington Barracks under the command of Colonel Manningham*. The members of the Experimental Corps of Riflemen were obliged to present rigid and unswerving obedience to orders received, in order to be more autonomous on the battlefield and to forge a special relationship based on mutual trust with their officers/NCOs. A new sense of comradeship was strengthened and one soldier of merit was selected in each half-platoon and promoted to corporal rank to assume command of the squad when NCOs were absent. In total, the Experimental Corps of Riflemen comprised five companies. Each was divided into two equal platoons, and each platoon into two squads. The members of each squad trained and lived together to forge bonds that would be of value when on the battlefield. Meritocracy was encouraged and prizes were offered by the officers to the best marksmen under their command.

Training the new experimental corps was intensive and comprised field exercises that were made as realistic as possible. The basic idea was that of training soldiers who could think in an autonomous way and act rapidly according to circumstances. Individual capabilities were fundamental in this regard. Training included moving swiftly on broken terrain, surviving with limited food rations, skirmishing on the open field, penetrating the enemy's lines without being noticed, launching surprise attacks to occupy enemy outposts, scouting for larger units during an advance and acting as rearguard to cover a retreat.

The new riflemen were given dark green uniforms and black leather equipment. In August 1800, after just a few months of training, three companies of the Experimental Corps of Riflemen joined an amphibious expedition launched against the Spanish arsenal of Ferrol. The mission was ultimately a failure for the British Army, but during operations the companies of riflemen fought with great competence and covered the retreat of the line infantrymen.

Private of the 1st Battalion/95th Rifles. (Photo and © 1/95th Rifles Living History Society)

After the return of the three companies to Britain, new recruits were added to the Rifle Corps (as it became known from October 1800). These recruits mostly came from fencible or volunteer regiments. In February 1801, it was transferred to the official establishment of the infantry and became a permanent unit; in 1802, it was officially transformed into a regiment and received the denomination of 95th Rifle Regiment.

During the following years, the riflemen took part in all the most important campaigns fought by the British Army, always distinguishing themselves and winning an impressive amount of awards. Due to their superior training and morale, they were usually employed as special forces. In 1805, a 2nd Battalion was added to the Rifle Regiment, followed by a 3rd Battalion in 1809. The two new units underwent the same training as the original and acquired the same special status. The only other unit of the British Army that was comparable in terms of quality was the 5th Battalion of the 60th Foot.

95th Rifle Regiment at war

The **1st Battalion of the 95th Foot** sent one of its companies to Denmark in 1801, and during 1805 it participated in the military operations taking place in Hanover, which was occupied by Napoleon's troops.

- In 1807, five companies of the battalion participated in an unlucky expedition sent to South America. All were captured during an assault against Buenos Aires.
- During 1808, all ten companies were sent to the Iberian Peninsula, where they fought with enormous valour until 1814.
- Due to heavy casualties, in 1810, the companies were reduced to eight and then to six in 1813. During that year, one company participated in operations in the Netherlands.
- In 1815, the entire battalion took part in the Belgian Campaign and fought at Waterloo.

- The **2nd Battalion**, created from drafts chosen from line regiments as well as from volunteers coming from the militia, participated in the South American Campaign of 1806–07 with three companies (that were all captured).
- In 1808, eight companies were sent to the Iberian Peninsula, before participating in the Walcheren Campaign during the following year.
- Between 1810 and 1814, several companies of the battalion were sent to the Iberian Peninsula; two participated in operations in the Netherlands during 1813–14.
- During 1815, six companies took part in the Belgian Campaign and fought at Waterloo; the battalion was the first British unit to enter Paris after the defeat of Napoleon.
- The **3rd Battalion**, created from drafts of the two existing battalions, participated with three companies in the Peninsular War during 1810–14.
- Two companies were sent to the Netherlands during 1813–14, while the remaining five participated in the War of 1812 against the United States (taking part in the disastrous Battle of New Orleans in 1815). Two companies of the battalion also participated in the Battle of Waterloo.

Training the light infantry

The early success of the Rifles encouraged the British high command to implement its light infantry reforms, by transforming several existing line regiments into light ones. The main supporter of this process was General Sir John Moore (1761–1809), who was ordered by the Duke of York to re-train the 43rd and 52nd regiments as light units. Moore, as commander of the 52nd unit, had always wished to expand the light component of the British foot troops. During 1803, the two chosen regiments were transferred to the training camp of the Rifles at Shorncliffe, Kent, where they trained with the 95th Regiment and were gradually transformed into light infantry corps.

This change did not affect the internal structure of the battalion, which continued to be based on those with ten companies. Instead, it affected its tactics and combat doctrines. The new light infantrymen retained their red uniforms and continued to be armed with smoothbore muskets (albeit of a special light version) but learned how to fight in open order and how to act as skirmishers. From this point forwards, the British Army started to comprise two distinct components of light foot troops: the elite Rifles, who were armed with rifled carbines and who were mostly employed as special forces, and the light infantrymen of the converted regiments, who were equipped with smoothbore muskets and were trained as light skirmishers.

The methods of training employed by Moore were very similar to those introduced by Manningham in 1800, which were based on the *Regulations for the Exercise of Riflemen and Light Infantry* published by the commander of the 60th Regiment's 5th Battalion (the Swiss Baron the Rottenburg, a light infantry expert). From July 1803, the three units training at Shorncliffe were united to form a Corps of Light Infantry commanded by Moore. In September 1805, the re-training of the 43rd and 52nd Foot was completed and both units were later sent to the Iberian Peninsula. Here, together with most of the 95th Rifles and with some allied units, they formed a special light division that acted as Wellington's special corps. The light division was structured on two brigades, comprising the following units:

1st Brigade
1st Battalion of the 43rd Foot Regiment
1st Battalion of the 95th (Rifle) Regiment
3rd Battalion of the 95th (Rifle) Regiment (just five companies)
3rd Battalion of the Portuguese Caçadores

2nd Brigade
1st Battalion of the 52nd Foot Regiment

2nd Battalion of the 95th (Rifle) Regiment
1st Battalion of the Portuguese 17th Line Infantry Regiment
2nd Battalion of the Portuguese 17th Line Infantry Regiment
1st Battalion of the Portuguese Caçadores

Following the operational success of the 43rd and 52nd Foot, during the Napoleonic Wars more line infantry units were transformed into light regiments. By 1815, the following regiments of the British infantry had become light ones (most of which were re-trained by Baron the Rottenburg):

51st Regiment of Foot, transformed in 1809
68th Regiment of Foot, transformed in 1808
71st Regiment of Foot, transformed in 1809
85th Regiment of Foot, transformed in 1808
90th Regiment of Foot, transformed in 1815

By the end of the Napoleonic period, the British Army comprised the following light units:

- one regiment of rifles (with three battalions)
- one mixed regiment of rifles/light infantry (with eight battalions)
- seven regiments of light infantry (former line units).

Light infantry at war

The former line units fought with great distinction during several campaigns:

Private of the King's German Legion rifles in 1815. (ASKB)

- The **43rd Foot** had its **1st Battalion** in the Iberian Peninsula from 1808 to 1814, after disbandment of the light division. It participated in the Battle of New Orleans against the United States.
- The **2nd Battalion** fought in Spain during 1808 and at Walcheren during 1809.
- The **51st Foot** took part in the Peninsular War from 1809 and continued to serve under Wellington until 1814, except for a brief interruption during 1809 (when it was sent to Walcheren). In 1815, it fought at Waterloo.
- The **52nd Foot** had its **1st Battalion** in Sicily during 1806–07; this was later sent to the Iberian Peninsula in 1809, where it remained until 1814. The unit also participated in the Battle of Waterloo.
- The **2nd Battalion** was in Spain during 1808–12, except for the brief interlude to the Walcheren Campaign. In 1813–14, it participated in military operations in the Netherlands.
- The **68th Foot** was in Walcheren during 1809, and in Spain during 1812–14.
- The **1st Battalion of the 71st Foot** participated in the Walcheren campaign of 1809 after a period of service in Spain. Later it was returned to the Iberian Peninsula, where it remained until 1814, after which it took part in the Battle of Waterloo.
- The **2nd Battalion** remained in Britain.
- The **85th Foot** was in Walcheren before being dispatched to Spain, where it served during 1811 and 1813. In 1814, it went to North America and participated in the War of 1812 against the United States, and also in the Battle of New Orleans in 1815.
- The **90th Foot** became a light regiment when the Belgian campaign of 1815 was over.

Chapter 5
The Life Guards and the Horse Guards

Like all the major European military forces of the Napoleonic period, the British incorporated cavalry units with guard status. These acted as the mounted bodyguard of the royal family and were the elite of the British heavy cavalry. In 1800, there were three guard corps of the British mounted troops: the 1st Regiment of Life Guards, the 2nd Regiment of Life Guards and the Royal Horse Guards.

The Life Guards

The Life Guards began in 1658, when England and Scotland were independent realms but ruled by the same monarch; as a result, they were originally part of the English Army. The 1st Troop of Life Guards was raised in 1658 as part of the military forces organised by Charles II during his exile in the Spanish Netherlands. At that time, the Stuart monarch was in exile outside his kingdom and raised a cavalry corps from his most loyal followers. During the same year, a 2nd Troop of Life Guards was organised, with the official denomination of The Duke of York's Troop of Horse Guards. A 3rd Troop of Life Guards was added in 1659, and was commonly known as Monck's Life Guards for the role that the unit had as mounted bodyguard to George Monck (1608–1670), the main political supporter of Charles II during the period of exile. The members of the three Life Guard units were known as gentlemen, since they all came from the higher social classes in England and were required to provide their own horses and uniforms. In 1660, with the Restoration of the Monarchy, the Life Guards were absorbed into the reorganised English Army and continued to act as the mounted bodyguard of the king. In 1678, one company of horse grenadiers was added to each troop of Life Guards; this was made up of rank and file soldiers rather than gentlemen.

The internal composition of a troop of Life Guards was as follows: one captain, four lieutenants, one cornet, one guidon, one quartermaster, four brigadiers, four sub-brigadiers, four trumpeters, one kettledrummer and 200 gentlemen.

Horse Guards

During the last quarter of the 17th century, horse grenadiers became quite popular in the European armies, together with their foot equivalents. Hand grenades were of common use during pitched battles and were employed to destroy the field fortifications built by the enemy. Very soon it became clear that the soldiers tasked with throwing hand grenades during battles required specific training. In addition, they were chosen from the tallest and fittest recruits of the units. As a result, the best soldiers in each infantry company started to be trained and equipped as grenadiers. Later they were assembled into independent companies or battalions and became a new and stable component of the European armies.

Around 1670, the first corps of horse grenadiers started to appear in some armies. These were not truly cavalry units, since their members acted as a sort of mounted infantrymen: they used their horses to travel long distances but usually dismounted to fight. It was practically impossible, in fact, to throw hand grenades from horseback. With the addition of the three companies of horse grenadiers, the numerical

Trooper (left) and officer (right) of the Life Guards wearing M1797 uniform. (ASKB)

establishment of the Horse Guard became significantly larger. The gentlemen did not have a high opinion of their plebeian comrades, despite the important tactical support they provided to the traditional cavalry.

The companies of horse grenadiers had two lieutenants, two sergeants, two corporals, two drummers, four hautboys and 64 privates.

In 1686, a 4th Troop of Life Guards, with an attached company of horse grenadiers, was raised by James II as part of a larger expansion of the English Army. In addition to the four units described above, there was also a Scottish corps of Life Guards. This was formed by Viscount Newburgh shortly after the Restoration of Charles II in 1661. Originally, the unit had an establishment with four officers, five NCOs, one surgeon, one clerk, three trumpeters, one kettledrummer and 120 troopers. A Scottish 2nd Troop of Life Guards was raised soon after the first, but this had a very short history since it was disbanded in 1676. During James II's reign (1665–68), Ireland had an independent Troop of Life Guards, which had an attached company of grenadiers. This was quartered in Dublin and was to act as the mounted bodyguard of the king when he was in Ireland.

Reorganising the Life Guards

With the outbreak of the Glorious Revolution and the landing of William of Orange in England, the internal organisation of the Life Guards was changed significantly. The armies of England, Scotland and Ireland remained independent from each other, but the new English king rationalised their internal structures. The English 4th Troop of Life Guards, only recently formed by James II, was disbanded in 1689. During the following ten years, it was replaced by a military unit from the Netherlands that was on English pay – the Garde du Corp. William of Orange was the supreme ruler of the Netherlands and his invasion force was mostly made up of Dutch military units. Being unsure of the loyalty of his new subjects, William retained several Dutch units on English pay long after the end of his Glorious Revolution. The Garde du Corps, also known as 4th Troop of Life Guards, returned to their homeland in 1699. The Scottish Life Guards remained loyal to James II during the Glorious Revolution, so most of them resigned their military positions; William of Orange, however, soon reorganised the unit with new gentlemen who were loyal to his cause. The troop of Irish Life Guards, instead, was disbanded since its members followed James II in exile and continued to serve the deposed monarch in France (as part of his army in exile). In 1709, the English and Scottish armies were merged to form the new British Army. As a result, the Scottish and English Life Guards when merged became the new 4th Troop of Life Guards.

Meanwhile, in 1693, the three troops of English horse grenadiers had been assembled into a single unit known as Horse Grenadier Guards. It was now a single troop and completely independent from the gentlemen of the Life Guards. In 1702, a troop of horse grenadiers was raised in Scotland and attached to the Scottish Life Guards. When the unit became part of the British Army in 1709, it was detached again and became an independent unit. As a result, the new British Army had a 1st and 2nd Troop of Horse Grenadiers in addition to the four troops of Life Guards. Since their foundation, the units of Life Guards had a distinctive heavy cavalry nature. Over time, this was acquired by the troops of horse grenadiers, who abandoned the use of hand grenades and became ordinary heavy cavalry units.

In 1746, the 3rd and 4th Troop of Life Guards were disbanded, following the outbreak of the Jacobite Rebellion that ravaged Scotland. In 1788, as part of the great organisational changes that took place after the British military defeat in the American Revolution, it was decided to assemble the two remaining troops of Life Guards with the two troops of Horse Grenadiers in order to form two consolidated regiments: the 1st Regiment of Life Guards and the 2nd Regiment of Life Guards. The first was formed by assembling the 1st Troop of Life Guards and the 1st Troop of Horse Grenadiers; the second was created by merging the 2nd Troop of Life Guards and the 2nd Troop of Horse Grenadiers. With this important organisational change, the nature of the Life Guards changed. The two new regiments started to comprise ordinary soldiers. Most of the aristocrats serving in the Life Guards were pensioned off and as a result, the two new units started to comprise common soldiers who had distinguished themselves for their valour and discipline. Both the 1st Regiment of Life Guards and the 2nd Regiment of Life Guards served with distinction during the Napoleonic Wars.

Until 1812, the Life Guards did not play an active part in the military campaigns that were fought by Britain against Napoleon. Since their foundation in 1788, in fact, both units had never participated in any overseas military campaign. In 1812, the two regiments were assembled into a Household Brigade and were sent to the Iberian Peninsula. Heret, Wellington fought the French, at the head of a large portion of the British Army. After spending six months in Lisbon, performing only ceremonial duties and improving combat training, the Household Brigade was finally employed against the French during 1813.

Trooper (left) and officer (right) of the Horse Guards wearing M1797 uniform. (ASKB)

Life Guards at war

- In 1813, the Life Guards took part in the important Battle of Vittoria, which saw the defeat of Napoleon's brother Joseph Bonaparte and the demise of his rule over Spain.
- In 1814, with the rest of the Peninsular Army, the Life Guards crossed the Pyrenees and invaded southern France to participate in the Battle of Toulouse, but did not conduct any glorious charge against the enemy. Wellington preferred to employ his battle-hardened regiments of veterans instead of the relatively inexperienced guardsmen. As a result, they were generally kept in reserve during major engagements and continued to have few opportunities to show their valour.
- In 1815, with the return of Napoleon from his exile, the Household Brigade was re-formed and sent to Belgium to stop the advance of the French. At Wellington's orders, the Life Guards participated in the decisive Battle of Waterloo. This time they had the opportunity to fight. During the early

phases of the clash, the **1st Regiment of Life Guards** counter-charged against the famous Lancers of Napoleon's Imperial Guard: this action saved some British cavalry units from destruction and bolstered the martial spirit of the Life Guards. Later, during the battle, the two regiments of Life Guards launched a massive cavalry charge against the French lines, which was a real success. The British cavalrymen routed the enemy infantry, captured two Eagles (ie, Imperial standards) from the French, put 15 enemy guns out of action and reached the French wagon train. The charge of the Life Guards was a key factor behind Wellington's victory at Waterloo, but it should be remembered that after breaking the enemy lines, the British cavalrymen lost their previous cohesion and experienced serious difficulties in returning to their starting position. Nevertheless, Household Brigade had won its first laurels on the battlefield and had finally shown to the world that it had great combat capabilities. During the following decades, it was employed again as a real military corps and not just as a ceremonial force to be seen during parades.

The Blues

The Royal Horse Guards, commonly known as the Blues because of their distinctive dark blue uniforms, had a completely different history to the two regiments of Life Guards. In 1650, while Oliver Cromwell

Trooper of the Life Guards wearing M1812 uniform. (ASKB)

was at the peak of his personal power, a heavy cavalry unit known as the Regiment of Cuirassiers was raised by Sir Arthur Haselrig, the parliamentary opposition leader to Charles I. From its formation, this corps had elite status and was mostly employed for escort duties as well as for policing. It performed the same main functions as the later French Gendarmerie. With the Restoration of Charles II, in 1660, the Regiment of Cuirassiers was transferred to royal service and most of its officers who were still loyal to the Parliamentarist cause were replaced by service personnel who were loyal to the Stuarts. The unit initially consisted of just three troops, whose members were mostly wealthy gentlemen. By the outbreak of the Glorious Revolution, however, it had eight troops and had received the new official denomination of The King's Regiment of Horse. Shortly before the outbreak of the Glorious Revolution, the corps received guard status, but when William of Orange disembarked in England, its members abandoned James II and sided with the Dutch pretender to the English throne.

During the early decades of the 18th century, the regiment continued to serve mostly as a police corps, garrisoning several areas of Britain and preventing the outbreak of local rebellions. In 1743, following Britain's involvement in the Austrian War of Succession that ravaged continental Europe, the corps fought with distinction at the Battle of Dettingen. The British military forces that were sent across the English Channel to fight against France comprised, for the first time, a Household Brigade made up of elements from the Life Guards and the Horse Grenadiers as well as from the future Royal Horse Guards (at that time, the Royal Horse Guards were still simply known by the name of their commanding colonel). At Dettingen, the Household Brigade showed great discipline and courage but could do very little to determine the outcome of the ongoing military events. In 1745, the Blues participated in the Battle of Fontenoy, during which they suffered heavy casualties resulting in defeat of the British military forces.

From 1750, the Blues received their new official denomination of Regiment of Royal Horse Guards, which defined them when they fought in the Seven Years' War. During that conflict, the unit distinguished itself in three important battles: Minden (1759), Warburg (1760) and Villinghausen (1761). When the regiment returned to Britain in 1763, at the end of the hostilities, it had lost most of its best elements due to the heavy casualties suffered. As a result, the Royal Horse Guards were reorganised. In 1788, after spending several years patrolling the countryside of the East Midlands, the Royal Horse Guards were transferred to London as a result of the reorganisation of the Life Guards' units. At this point, the government was not completely sure about the reliability of the new regiments of reorganised Life Guards and deployed the Blues in the capital to count on their experience. Until that moment, the Royal Horse Guards had mostly been employed to perform internal police duties but had also seen substantial fighting overseas. In 1793, after the outbreak of war with Revolutionary France, the Blues were sent to continental Europe and took part in the military operations that were fought in Flanders. Despite the many difficulties encountered, the Royal Horse Guards showed all their discipline and valour during this new campaign. However, it was a failure for the British Army and for their allies since Belgium and the Netherlands were ultimately occupied by the French.

In 1800, new barracks were built for the Royal Horse Guards in Windsor and so the unit started to perform as mounted bodyguard for the royal family on a permanent basis. Formally, the regiment received the same special status as the Life Guards only in 1820.

The Blues at war

- In 1812, the Blues contributed to the formation of the Household Brigade together with the Life Guards and were sent to the Iberian Peninsula. Here, at Wellington's orders they participated in the Battle of Vittoria but were prevented from conducting a charge against the French by the morphology of the local terrain.
- In 1814, with the rest of the Peninsular Army, the Royal Horse Guards returned to Britain. Very soon, however, they were re-mobilised along with the other units of the Household Brigade due to Napoleon's return to France. The Blues participated with great distinction in the Battle of Waterloo, during which they fought with against the French heavy cavalry. In particular, the Royal Horse Guards counter-charged against the enemy Cuirassiers, who were considered to be the best heavy cavalry of continental Europe. The Blues showed that they were second to none in terms of courage and discipline, thus confirming their excellent reputation.

In 1820, the Royal Horse Guards, like the Life Guards, received new uniforms with cuirasses (a piece of armor covering the body from neck to waist) that were similar to those worn today; it should be noticed, however, that they had already used (albeit for a brief period) metal cuirasses some years before. This was in 1794, while the regiment was deployed to continental Europe to fight against the French; the soldiers of the unit, however, soon discarded their cuirasses because they were extremely uncomfortable to wear.

Unit structure

Generally, the mounted regiments of the British Army were structured on troops, with two of the troops making up a squadron. At the beginning of the Revolutionary Wars fought against France, the two regiments of Life Guards were organised into five troops each. A single troop comprised 150 soldiers, divided into three small companies of 50 men. Four troops were assembled together to form two active squadrons, while the remaining one acted as a sort of regimental depot. In 1799, a sixth troop was added to both regiments, to form a reserve squadron. The Royal Horse Guards were not part (at least officially) of the Royal Household and thus at the beginning of the Revolutionary Wars they had an internal establishment with eight troops, which was different from that of the two regiments of Life Guards. However, the Life Guards were reorganised with eight troops each (1812). The troops of the Life Guards

Trooper of the Life Guards (left) and trooper of the Horse Guards (right) in 1815.

still had only 50 troopers each, and thus their numerical consistency was smaller than that of the Horse Guards' troops. As a result, in 1809, both regiments of Life Guards comprised a total of 416 officers and men each, while the regiment of Horse Guards mustered a total of 654 officers and men. During 1812, the internal establishment of the Horse Guards was expanded to ten troops, but was reduced to eight with the demobilisation of 1814.

Above left: Trooper of the Horse Guards wearing M1812 uniform.

Above right: Trooper of the Horse Guards wearing M1812 uniform. (ASKB)

Before the outbreak of the Revolutionary Wars against France, each British line heavy cavalry regiment consisted of six troops that were assembled into three squadrons. Of the squadrons, one was a depot unit always kept in reserve in Britain and was never sent to serve overseas. The depot squadron of each regiment, in fact, had to provide new recruits with solid basic training in the two active squadrons in order to replenish the losses suffered during overseas deployments. In 1793, with the war mobilisation following the outbreak of hostilities with France, the standard establishment of a heavy cavalry regiment was increased from six to nine troops; this organisational change, however, was not immediately adopted by all units and several regiments continued to have a variable number of troops for some time. In 1800, the troops in each unit were increased to ten, in order to form four active squadrons and one depot squadron. During 1811, however, the number of active squadrons was reduced to three and the total number of troops in each regiment was fixed at eight (six active and two depot).

The standard regimental staff of the heavy cavalry units comprised the following elements: one colonel, two lieutenant-colonels, two majors, six captains, one captain-lieutenant, eight lieutenants, nine cornets, one paymaster, one adjutant, one surgeon, two assistant-surgeons and one veterinary surgeon.

The three guard units of the British cavalry had irregular regimental staff, whose composition varied a lot during the Napoleonic Wars. By 1815, they were as follows:

- The 1st Life Guards had one colonel, two supernumerary lieutenant-colonels, one major, eight captains, eight lieutenants, six cornets, one adjutant, one surgeon, two assistant-surgeons and two veterinary surgeons.
- The 2nd Life Guards had one colonel, two supernumerary lieutenant-colonels, one major, eight captains, eight lieutenants, seven cornets, one adjutant, two surgeons, one assistant-surgeon and two veterinary surgeons
- The Horse Guards had one colonel, two supernumerary lieutenant-colonels, two majors, ten captains, 11 lieutenants, eight cornets, one adjutant, one surgeon, two assistant-surgeons and two veterinary surgeons.

A standard heavy cavalry troop was made up of the following: one captain, one lieutenant-colonel, one major, one quartermaster (sergeant-major since 1809), four sergeants, four corporals, one trumpeter and 85 troopers. The troops of the Life Guards and of the Horse Guards continued to comprise a quartermaster also after 1809; in addition, they did not have sergeants.

Chapter 6
Dragoon Guards and Dragoons

A t the outbreak of the Revolutionary Wars, the British heavy cavalry consisted of two distinct categories of units: the Dragoon Guards and the Dragoons. The former were made up of heavy horsemen and the latter were made up of medium horsemen. In practice, however, there was very little difference between the two categories, since both were trained and equipped to act as shock cavalry. A tactical difference existed between them and the regiments of Light Dragoons (see next chapter).

The Dragoon Guards were created in 1746, when the general organisation of the British heavy cavalry underwent radical reform. The first two heavy cavalry units that received the new denomination of Dragoon Guards were the Queen's Own Regiment of Horse and the Earl of Peterborough's Regiment of Horse, which became the 1st Dragoon Guards and the 2nd Dragoon Guards, respectively. In 1747, a third unit, the Earl of Plymouth's Regiment of Horse, was converted into a regiment of Dragoon Guards. This was followed by another four units in 1788, when the British cavalry was again reorganised. By 1790, the British Army incorporated seven regiments of Dragoon Guards.

Since the days of the Restoration (1660), the English cavalry had been made up of horse regiments and of dragoon regiments. Horse regiments were equipped with cuirasses until the last decades of the 17th century and consisted of heavy cavalry. Dragoon regiments were originally raised as mounted infantry corps that were not tasked with conducting frontal charges. Initially, in fact, the dragoons were introduced in the European armies post-1648 as chosen units of infantrymen who could use horses to travel long distances or to move on the battlefield but who dismounted to fight. In practice, they consisted of infantrymen with a higher degree of mobility; this was clear from their personal equipment, since they were armed with long infantry muskets and did not have the same leather boots as the cavalrymen of the horse regiments. During the first decades of the 18th century, the dragoons gradually lost their original mounted infantry status and transformed into standard line cavalry. At the same time, the horse regiments discarded their metal cuirasses and started to use lighter personal equipment. As a result of these changes, the existing tactical differences that distinguished horse regiments from the dragoon ones practically ceased to exist. Both the heavy horsemen and the dragoons, in fact, did not wear cuirasses and were now employed to perform the same duties. In 1746, the British government transformed the horse regiments into dragoon ones in order to cut costs and eliminate a tactical differentiation that no longer existed in practice.

The heavy mounts of the horse regiments were a considerable cost but produced no real advantages during field battles. In addition, the soldiers of the horse regiments were better paid than those of the dragoon units. With the creation of the Dragoon Guards, the British government found a compromise. The costly horse regiments were abolished, but at the same time their members kept alive the traditions of the British heavy cavalry. The term 'Guards' as their new official denomination underlined that the units of Dragoon Guards were the elite of the British heavy cavalry and marked a formal difference between them and the standard dragoons. The transformation of the horse regiments into Dragoon Guards was very unpopular among the units affected, since it led to a drastic reduction in pay. In addition, the new official denomination did not signify the inclusion of the former horse regiments into the Royal

Household. In practice, the Dragoon Guards had a niche between the Life Guards/Horse Guards and the standard regiments of dragoons. By the outbreak of the Revolutionary Wars, the dragoons had six regiments. As a result, the whole heavy cavalry of the British Army comprised a total of 13 regiments (reduced to 12 from 1799).

1st Dragoon Guards

Raised in 1685, the 1st Dragoon Guards was originally named as the Queen's Own Regiment of Horse in honour of Queen Mary (1658–1718), the consort of James II. With the outbreak of the Glorious Revolution, it joined William of Orange's cause, taking part in the Battle of the Boyne (1690) and the following Battle of Aughrim (1691). Shortly before the founding of the British Army, it participated in all the most important battles fought by Marlborough during the War of the Spanish Succession: Blenheim (1704), Ramilies (1706), Oudenarde (1708) and Malplaquet (1709). In 1714, with the arrival of the House of Hanover in Great Britain, it was renamed as the 2nd King's Own Regiment of Horse in honour of the new King, George I. With this new denomination, the unit took part in the Battle of Dettingen in 1743, during the War of

the Austrian Succession. Following the outbreak of the Jacobite Rebellion in Scotland, it was transformed into the 1st Regiment of Dragoon Guards. In 1760, during the Seven Years' War, the corps distinguished itself at the Battle of Corbach and at the Battle of Warburg (1760). In 1793, with the outbreak of war with France, its internal establishment was augmented from nine to 12 troops; only half of which were sent to continental Europe to fight against the French. After taking part with distinction in the Flanders Campaign, the troops of the regiment were reduced to seven (1795). During 1798, one troop was added to the regiment, followed by another two in 1800. During the following ten years, the unit remained garrisoned in England or Ireland and was expanded to 12 troops. During 1814, two troops were temporarily disbanded but were soon raised again when Napoleon returned to France after his first exile. Finally, after many years of inactivity, the regiment was sent to Belgium in 1815 and participated with distinction in the British cavalry charges at Waterloo.

2nd Dragoon Guards

Raised in 1685, this regiment was originally named as the Earl of Peterborough's Regiment of Horse. With the outbreak of the Glorious Revolution, its members joined William of Orange's cause, taking part in the Battle of the Boyne and in the following Battle of Aughrim. During the War of the Spanish Succession, it was sent to Portugal to fight against the Bourbon military forces operating in the Iberian Peninsula, taking part in the Battle of Almenar (1710). After returning home, the regiment contributed to the suppression of the 1715 Jacobite rising. In 1746, following the new Jacobite rising that was crushed with the Battle of Culloden, it became the 2nd Regiment of Dragoon Guards. In 1760, during the Seven Years' War, the corps distinguished itself at the Battle of Corbach and at the Battle of Warburg. Later, during

Officer of the 1st Dragoon Guards wearing M1797 uniform. (ASKB)

the same conflict, it fought brilliantly at the Battle of Wilhelmsthal (1762). In 1793, with the outbreak of war with France, its internal establishment was augmented from nine to 12 troops; though only ten were sent to continental Europe to fight against the French. After taking part, with distinction, in the Flanders Campaign, the troops of the regiment were reduced to eight (1795). In 1799, two troops were added to the regiment, but were later disbanded in 1802 during the reorganisation of the British Army that followed the signing of the Peace of Amiens. In 1806, the number of troops was increased again to ten; three years later, six troops from the regiment participated in the unlucky Walcheren Campaign in the Netherlands. In 1813, eight of the ten troops were prepared for service in the Iberian Peninsula, though they did not embark. During 1814, two of the regiment's troops were temporarily disbanded, but they were soon re-raised when Napoleon returned to France after his first exile. The unit was sent to Belgium but did not arrive in time to fight at Waterloo; instead it remained on the continent as part of the British Army of Occupation.

3rd Dragoon Guards
Raised in 1685, the 3rd Dragoon Guards was originally named as the Earl of Plymouth's Regiment of Horse. After the Glorious Revolution, it served with distinction during the War of the Spanish Succession. The regiment took part in the following battles: Schellenberg (1704), Blenheim (1704), Ramilies (1706), Oudenarde (1708) and Malplaquet (1709). In 1747, it was transformed into the 3rd Regiment of Dragoon Guards. After taking part in the Flanders Campaign against Revolutionary France, the unit remained garrisoned in England or Ireland until being dispatched to the Iberian Peninsula in 1809.

4th Dragoon Guards
Raised in 1685, this regiment was originally the Earl of Arran's Regiment of Horse. With the outbreak of the Glorious Revolution, it joined William of Orange's cause, taking part in the Battle of the Boyne and in some subsequent actions that took place in Ireland. In 1746, the unit was transferred to the Irish establishment of the British Army, where it remained until being transferred back to the English establishment in 1788. In that same year, it became the 4th Regiment of Dragoon Guards (Royal Irish).

At the beginning of the Revolutionary Wars, the number of troops in the unit was expanded to nine. In 1798, it contributed to the crushing of the Irish Rebellion, supported by France. In 1800, the regiment was expanded to ten troops, but this organisational change was quite short-lived since the unit was reduced to just eight troops in 1802. After spending several years in England, guarding the countryside and suppressing local riots, the 4th Dragoon Guards were again expanded to ten troops and were ordered to send six of them to Portugal (1811). During the year 1812, the regiment fought at Ciudad Rodrigo and Badajoz, Spain. After returning home in March 1813, it did not take part in any other combat action until the end of the Napoleonic Wars.

5th Dragoon Guards
Raised in 1686, the 5th Dragoon Guards was originally named as the Earl of Shrewsbury's Regiment of Horse. With the outbreak of the Glorious Revolution, it joined William of Orange's cause, taking part in the Battle of the Boyne and in the First Siege of Limerick (1690). During the long War of the Spanish Succession, the regiment took part in the Battle of Blenheim as well as to those of Ramilies and Malplaquet. During the following 80 years, it remained garrisoned in Ireland, without seeing action in continental Europe. In 1788, the corps became the new 5th Regiment of Dragoon Guards. Five years later, it was sent to Flanders where it participated in the military campaign fought against Revolutionary France.

Officer of the 6th Dragoon Guards wearing M1797 uniform. (ASKB)

With its internal establishment of ten troops, the regiment was one of the British military units that crushed the Irish Rebellion of 1798. For a short period, during 1802–03, the number of troops was reduced from ten to eight. During 1811, six of the ten troops were sent to Portugal. In 1812, they participated with distinction in the decisive Battle of Salamanca. During 1813, the 5th Dragoon Guards continued to serve in the Iberian Peninsula, fighting at Vittoria. In 1814, the regiment followed Wellington in his invasion of southern France and took part in the Battle of Toulouse. Reduced to just eight troops, the unit returned to Britain and did not take part in the Belgian Campaign of 1815.

6th Dragoon Guards

Raised in 1686, it was originally named as Lord Lumley's Regiment of Horse. With the outbreak of the Glorious Revolution, it joined William of Orange's cause and went to Ireland to fight the Jacobite military forces. Later, it was sent to continental Europe and participated in the War of the Grand Alliance (1688–97), which was fought between France and a large multinational coalition of states that comprised England. In 1692, the unit was renamed the King's Regiment of Carabineers and with this denomination it took part in the War of the Spanish Succession. During that conflict, it fought at Blenheim and at Ramilies. In 1745, it was part of the British military forces that crushed the Jacobite rising. Some years later, it was transferred to the Irish establishment of the British Army. It remained there until 1788, when it was transferred back to the English establishment and transformed into the 6th Regiment of Dragoon Guards. In 1793, it was sent to continental Europe and saw action against the French in Flanders, where it fought with distinction. During 1796–1807, the unit was garrisoned in Ireland and took part in the bloody repression of the 1798 Irish Rebellion. In 1806, a detachment of 400 officers and men from the 6th Dragoon Guards was sent to South America and took part in a British expedition organised against Buenos Aires (at that time Argentina was a colony of Spain, which was an ally of Napoleon). This attack, which was followed by a similar one in 1807, was a failure. After this overseas mission, the regiments remained garrisoned in England and Ireland until the end of the Napoleonic Wars (thus not taking part in any major engagement against the French).

7th Dragoon Guards

Raised in 1688, the 7th Dragoon Guards was originally named Lord Cavendish's Regiment of Horse. Despite being organised to provide a mounted escort for Princess Anne, the younger daughter of James II, the unit soon joined William of Orange when he landed in England. During the so-called Williamite Wars fought in Ireland between the new English monarch and the Jacobite rebels, the regiment took part in the Battle of the Boyne before being sent to continental Europe. Here it participated in the Grand Alliance War and operated against the French military forces of Louis XIV. The corps returned to continental Europe with the outbreak of the Spanish Succession War; during which it fought with distinction at Blenheim, Elixheim, Ramilies and Malplaquet. After the end of the hostilities, the unit spent several years in Ireland where it acted as a garrison corps. In 1742, the horsemen of the regiment were sent to Flanders, following the outbreak of the War of the Austrian Succession. During this conflict they participated in the Battle of Dettingen and the Battle of Fontenoy. After another period as garrison in Ireland, the unit was sent to continental Europe to fight in the Seven Years' War; and participated with distinction to the Battle of Warburg. In 1788, it was transformed into the 7th Regiment of Dragoon Guards and during the following years it remained garrison in England and Ireland. In 1798, it was part of the British military forces that crushed the Irish Rebellion. During the Napoleonic, Wars it remained at home.

Officers of the King's German Legion heavy cavalry.

Analysing the regimental histories of the seven regiments of Dragoon Guards, it is possible to find some common elements. First of all, these units were all organised during the reign of James II and most of them were raised for countering the Monmouth Rebellion that broke out in 1685. Until their transformation into Dragoon Guards corps, these regiments participated in all the major battles fought by Great Britain on the continent during the 18th century (War of the Spanish Succession, War of the Austrian Succession and Seven Years' War). From 1788, these regiments were only sent to serve overseas on very rare occasions and thus spent most of their regimental life as garrison corps in Great Britain. Most notably, the Dragoon Guards were deployed in Ireland where they were tasked with patrolling the countryside and preventing the outbreak of local uprisings. The British government considered the Dragoon Guards as a 'strategic reserve' and preferred to keep them at home. These horsemen had the necessary training and expertise to act like the contemporary French Gendarmerie (reorganised as a 'military police' corps after the outbreak of the French Revolution). This trend was confirmed during the Napoleonic Period.

As we will see from their regimental histories, the units of dragoons were employed much more frequently in combat than the Dragoon Guards (especially during the Napoleonic Wars):

1st Dragoons

This regiment, the oldest dragoon unit of the British Army, was organised in 1661, shortly after the Restoration of Charles II, from veterans of the disbanded Parliamentary Army. Initially, it consisted of just one troop, but was later expanded to four before being sent to serve in Tangier. Located on the coastline of Morocco, Tangier was an English colony between 1661–84 and required a garrison in order to be defended from England's colonial rivals. The four troops of dragoons, collectively known as 'Tangier Horse', served in Morocco until 1678 and were later

Trooper of the 1st Dragoon Guards wearing M1812 uniform.

sent to Scotland to police the local Covenanters (a Presbyterian movement that caused some political troubles for the central government).

In 1680, the unit was disbanded and its men were sent back to Tangiers as reinforcements for the local garrison. Three years later, they returned to England and were reorganised as an independent regiment of dragoons. This was expanded to six troops and assumed the new denomination of The Royal Regiment of Dragoons. Like most of the English military units, after the outbreak of the Glorious Revolution it became part of the Williamite Army and, as such, it participated in the Battle of the Boyne and to the First Siege of Limerick. During the War of the Austrian Succession, it participated in the Battle of Dettingen and the Battle of Fontenoy. In 1751, it assumed the definitive denomination of 1st Royal Regiment of Dragoons. The unit took part in the Seven Years' War and fought with distinction at the Battle of Warburg in 1760. With the outbreak of the hostilities with Revolutionary France, the corps sent four of its ten troops to Flanders. During 1796–1801, the regiment remained in garrison on the coastline of southern England, where it mostly performed anti-smuggler duties. For a brief period, during 1802–03, its internal establishment was reduced from ten to eight troops. In January 1807, the unit was transferred to Ireland, where it remained until 1809. During summer of that year, eight troops from the regiment were sent to the Iberian Peninsula. Here they remained until 1813, taking part in several minor combat actions and then being temporarily reduced to six in 1811. After participating in Wellington's invasion of southern France in 1814, the 1st Dragoons were permanently reduced to six troops.

In 1815, the regiment was made part of the famous 'Union Brigade' and was sent to continental Europe to participate in the Belgian Campaign. Together with the 2nd and 6th Dragoons, the 1st Dragoons participated in the famous cavalry charge that stabilised the British front during the Battle of Waterloo. The troopers of the unit distinguished themselves during the fight, since they captured the Imperial Eagle of a French line infantry regiment. The nickname Union Brigade derived from the fact that it was made up of regiments from different areas of the United Kingdom: the 1st Dragoons from England, the 2nd Dragoons from Scotland and the 6th Dragoons from Ireland.

2nd Dragoons

This regiment was raised in 1678 as three independent troops of dragoons that were part of the Scots Army. At that time, Scotland still had an independent army that was mostly used to perform internal police duties. In 1681, another three troops of dragoons were raised and assembled with the existing ones to form a new unit that assumed the denomination of Royal Regiment of Scots Dragoons. During this early phase of its history, the unit was already mounted on grey horses and thus later received its famous nickname of 'Scots Greys'. With the outbreak of the Glorious Revolution, like the rest of the Scots Army, the Royal Regiment of Scots Dragoons sided with William of Orange and helped him crush the revolt of the Scottish Jacobites. During the War of the Spanish Succession, as part of the Scots Army, the unit fought on Marlborough's orders with great distinction. At that time, the dragoons were still mostly employed as mounted infantrymen and as such they participated in the following battles: Schellenberg, Blenheim, Elixheim, Ramilies, Oudenarde and Malplaquet. After assuming the new denomination of Royal North British Dragoons, the regiment was absorbed like the rest of the Scots Army into the new British one.

After returning to their homeland, the Scots Greys remained loyal to the House of Hanover when the Jacobite rising of 1715 began. The Scottish dragoons fought with great determination against the rebels and were one of the key factors behind the final victory of the British military forces. After the end of the rising in 1719, the regiment remained garrison in Scotland for more than two decades and continued to perform the main duty for which it had been created: policing Scotland and preventing the outbreak of risings among the Highland clans. In 1742, two years after the beginning of the War of the Austrian Succession, the Scots Greys were sent to Flanders to fight against the French. Like several other British cavalry units, the regiment fought at Dettingen in 1743 and at Fontenoy in 1745; during the latter clash, they covered the retreat of the defeated British infantry. When the Jacobite rising of 1745 began, the corps was not transferred to Scotland and remained to serve in Flanders until the end of the War of the Austrian Succession in 1748. During 1755, just for a very short period, a single company of light cavalry was added to the establishment of the regiment; this, however, was soon detached from it and became an independent corps. With the outbreak of the Seven Years' War, the Scots Greys were sent to Germany where they operated together with the military forces of Hanover. In 1759, the regiment participated in the clashes of Bergen and Minden, during which it had little opportunity to show its valour. During the following year, however, the Scots Greys conducted a brilliant frontal charge at the Battle of Warburg, which was decisive for the outcome of the clash. Before the end of the conflict, in 1762, the Scottish regiment took part in the Battle of Wilhelmsthal, during which it attacked the French troops after the latter had already been routed, capturing many prisoners and even part of the French baggage train. During the long period 1764–93, the Scots Greys remained in Britain, performing garrison duties and not taking part in any combat action.

In 1768, they replaced their distinctive mitre-style grenadier caps with the tall bearskins that they later wore at the Battle of Waterloo.

During this same period, one troop of light dragoons was attached to each troop of the regiment; this organisational change, however, lasted for just a few years, since, in 1779, all the detachments of light dragoons were assembled to form an independent unit of light cavalry. Before the outbreak of the hostilities with Revolutionary France, the Scots Greys were organised into five troops; when the war began, however, these were rapidly increased to nine. During 1793–94, the Scots Greys operated with the British expeditionary force that was deployed in Flanders, obtaining a remarkable victory over France at the Battle of Tournai. During that clash, the Scottish regiment broke the defensive formations of the enemy infantry, which was deployed in squares. In 1795, the four troops of the Scots Greys that had served in continental Europe returned home, where the whole regiment was reduced to eight troops. During the following years, despite the fact that Britain was fighting against Napoleon around the globe, the Scottish unit was never sent to serve overseas. When Bonaparte returned to France in 1815, however, the Scots Greys were mobilised and their internal establishment was increased to ten troops. Six of the these were sent to Belgium as part of the famous Union Brigade, a large heavy cavalry formation that comprised three regiments of dragoons. At Waterloo, the Scots Greys were deployed in the third line of Wellington's army, on the left flank. When Napoleon ordered a general advance of his infantry against the centre of the British forces, the Household Brigade and the Union Brigade received the order to counter-attack in order to stabilise the British force. The Scots Greys, however, were to remain back during the charge and to act as a reserve in case the attack failed. Seeing that the British infantry was going to be routed, the commander of the regiment charged. The charge of the regiment, which advanced at the cry 'Scotland forever!', was devastating for the French infantry, which was moving in open order and did not have time to form defensive squares.

During the furious assault, the Scottish soldiers captured the Imperial Eagle of an enemy infantry regiment. After routing the French troops that were attacking the British lines, the regiment continued its advance and found itself in front of the main French line. By now their horses were exhausted and their formation was disorganised; as a result, they were easily counter-charged by the French cuirassiers and lancers. The Union Brigade suffered very heavy losses during this phase of the battle and its commander, William Ponsonby (1772–1815), was killed. Under heavy French artillery fire and with the enemy cavalry in close pursuit, the British cavalrymen returned to their lines after having been severely punished. Their dramatic frontal charge, however, had saved Wellington's line from collapse and had determined the outcome of the Battle of Waterloo.

3rd Dragoons

Raised in 1685 as the Queen's Regiment of Dragoons, the 3rd Dragoons originally consisted of six troops and joined William of Orange when he landed in England at the outbreak of the Glorious Revolution. During 1690–91, the unit fought against the Jacobites in Ireland, before being sent to continental Europe to participate in the Grand Alliance War. With the beginning of the new century, the regiment was

Officer of the 2nd Dragoons (Royal Scots) wearing M1812 uniform. (ASKB)

sent to serve overseas due to the outbreak of the War of the Spanish Succession. During that conflict the corps was deployed to the Iberian Peninsula and participated in the bloody Battle of Almansa. In 1715, after returning home, it was made part of the British military forces that were tasked with suppressing the Jacobite rising. During the following decades, the regiment remained a garrison in southern England where it was mostly employed to counter smuggling. With the outbreak of the War of the Austrian Succession, the unit was sent to continental Europe, where it participated in the Battle of Dettingen and to the Battle of Fontenoy. With the outbreak of the new Jacobite rising, the corps was rapidly returned home and could participate in the decisive Battle of Culloden that saw the defeat of the Jacobites.

Until the outbreak of the Napoleonic Wars, the regiment did not see much action except for a few minor actions fought against the French during the Seven Years' War. The unit, in fact, did not take part in the Flanders Campaign of 1793–95. In 1809, it was selected to be part of the British expeditionary force that landed in Walcheren (Netherlands) where many of its members, like the rest of the British soldiers, were caught by the terrible disease known as 'Walcheren Fever' and died without seeing action against the French. In 1810, the regiment remained garrisoned in England and suppressed some local protests, before being sent to Portugal during the following year. In 1812, the 3rd Dragoons participated in the Siege of Ciudad Rodrigo and in the Siege of Badajoz; and charged against the French with success at the Battle of Salamanca. In 1813, the regiment was, at Wellington's orders, during the decisive Battle of Vittoria and in 1814, it took part in the British invasion of southern France (fighting at the Battle of Toulouse). After years of distinguished service in the Iberian Peninsula, the 3rd Dragoons returned home in 1814 and did not participate in the Belgian Campaign of 1815. In 1818, the unit was transformed into a regiment of Light Dragoons.

4th Dragoons

Raised in 1685 as Princess Anne of Denmark's Regiment of Dragoons, this regiment joined William of Orange soon after the outbreak of the Glorious Revolution. It was sent to Scotland where it fought against the local Jacobites and then to continental Europe where it participated in the War of the Grand Alliance (seeing action on several occasions in Flanders). During the War of the Spanish Succession, it was sent to the Iberian Peninsula and fought with determination at the bloody Battle of Almansa (1707). With the outbreak of the 1715 Jacobite Uprising, it was employed against the Scottish insurgents and took part in the Battle of Sheriffmuir. After many years spent at garrison in Britain, the unit returned to continental Europe with the outbreak of the War of the Austrian Succession. During that conflict, it participated in the Battle of Dettingen and in the Battle of Lauffeld (1747). During the American Revolution, the unit remained in Britain and took part in the suppression of the so-called Gordon Riots, which took place in London (1780). It remained at its base in Britain until 1809, when it was sent to the Iberian Peninsula. Here, it participated in the battles of Talavera (1809) and Albuera (1811). In 1812, it was at Salamanca and in 1813, it fought at Vittoria, always with great distinction. The regiment took part in the British invasion of southern France (1814) before returning home and being reduced from ten to eight troops. In 1818, it was transformed into a regiment of Light Dragoons.

5th Dragoons

Raised in 1689 as part of William of Orange's new English Army during the Glorious Revolution, it originally had the official denomination of Colonel Wynn's Regiment of Dragoons. In 1690, it participated in the Williamite Wars in Ireland, taking part in the Battle of the Boyne and in the Battle of Aughrim. In 1704, the unit was renamed as the Royal Dragoons of Ireland and was later sent to continental Europe to fight in the War of the Spanish Succession. During that conflict, it participated in: Blenheim, Ramilies, Oudenarde and Malplaquet. During the following decades the unit remained at its garrison in Ireland, where it patrolled the countryside preventing the outbreak of local revolts. With the outbreak of the Irish Rebellion in 1798, the 5th Dragoons played a crucial role in suppressing the activities of the insurgents and took part in the Battle of Enniscorthy. Before and after the Irish Rebellion, the regiment was dispersed in many small detachments across Ireland. This lack of regimental unity had extremely negative consequences for the morale of the corps, whose members were accused of treachery and sedition in 1799. After an official investigation, the regiment was disbanded during the last months of 1799 and was erased from the records of the British Army.

6th Dragoons

Raised in 1689 as part of William of Orange's new English Army during the Glorious Revolution, it originally had the official denomination of Richard Cunningham's Regiment of Dragoons. Very soon,

Trooper of the 2nd Dragoons (left) and trooper of the 3rd Dragoons (right) in 1815.

however, this unit received the famous nickname of Inniskilling Dragoons since it was quartered in Inniskilling Castle, Northern Ireland. In 1690, the regiment took part in the decisive Battle of the Boyne and later remained in Ireland for some time. When the Jacobite rising of 1715 began, it was transferred to Scotland where it fought against the Jacobites in the Battle of Sheriffmuir. With the outbreak of the War of the Austrian Secession it was transferred to continental Europe, where it participated in: Dettingen, Fontenoy, Rocoux and Lauffeld. During the Seven Years' War, the corps was sent to fight against France and took part in the engagements of Minden and Wetter (1759). During 1793–95, the 6th Dragoons were deployed in Flanders and participated in several actions that were fought against the French. In 1802–03, for just a few months, the internal establishment of the regiment was reduced from ten to eight troops. Until 1815, the unit remained at its garrison in Britain, spending most of the time in Ireland and being reduced to nine troops during 1814. When Napoleon returned to France, six troops of the 6th Dragoons were sent to Belgium where they participated in the Battle of Waterloo as part of the Union Brigade. Like the Scots Greys, this regiment distinguished itself during the cavalry charge that stabilised the British front.

It's clear that the dragoons of the British Army played an important role during the Napoleonic Wars, but their military contribution was important from a qualitative point of view more than from a quantitative one. It should be noted, in fact, that after the disbandment of the 5th Dragoons, the British Army had capacity to deploy only 12 heavy cavalry regiments. Of these, seven were of Guard Dragoons and were employed overseas only on rare occasions. The heavy cavalry of the British Army was always considered as a 'strategic reserve' and was kept at its garrison whenever possible. Its units were never sent to serve in the colonies, for example in the Thirteen Colonies when the American Revolution began; in addition, they participated in the continental wars fought by Britain in Europe only when absolutely necessary.

The regiments of Light Dragoons were sent to serve overseas much more frequently and were much more numerous than the heavy cavalry during the Napoleonic Period. From an organisational point of view, the regiments of Light Dragoons were numbered in progressive order after the six dragoons; as a result, so their first unit was the 7th Regiment of Light Dragoons.

The heavy cavalry regiments of the British Army were structured so that two troops made up a squadron. Squadrons were identified by letters, troops by numbers. Before the outbreak of the Revolutionary Wars against France, each British heavy cavalry regiment consisted of six troops assembled into three squadrons.

One squadron was a 'depot' unit that was always kept in reserve in Britain and was never sent to serve overseas. The depot squadron of each regiment had to provide new recruits with solid basic training to the two active squadrons in order to replenish losses suffered during overseas deployments. In 1793, with the war mobilisation following the outbreak of hostilities with France, the standard establishment of a heavy cavalry regiment was increased from six to nine troops (ten in some cases, such as the 1st Dragoon Guards or the 1st Dragoons). This organisational change was not adopted rapidly by all units and several regiments continued to have a variable number of troops for some time. In 1800, the troops in each unit were increased to ten, in order to form four active squadrons and one depot squadron. During 1811, however, the number of active squadrons was reduced to three and the total number of troops in each regiment was fixed at eight (six active and two depot). Again, this organisational change was not adopted rapidly by all.

Unit composition

The regimental staff of the heavy cavalry units comprised: one colonel, two lieutenant-colonels, two majors, six captains, one captain-lieutenant, eight lieutenants, nine cornets, one paymaster, one adjutant, one surgeon, two assistant-surgeons and one veterinary surgeon.

Each troop included: one captain, one lieutenant-colonel, one major, one quartermaster, four sergeants, four corporals, one trumpeter and 85 troopers. In June 1809, the quartermaster of each troop was transformed into a sergeant-major and a lieutenant-quartermaster was added to the staff of each regiment. During 1810, the internal composition of a heavy cavalry unit's regimental staff was partly modified and became: one colonel, one lieutenant-colonel, one major, one adjutant, one lieutenant-quartermaster, one paymaster, one surgeon, two assistant-surgeons, one veterinary surgeon and one regimental sergeant-major. The new composition of a single troop became: one captain, one lieutenant, one cornet, one troop sergeant-major, three sergeants, four corporals, one trumpeter, one farrier and 63 troopers. By 1809, the average numerical consistency of all heavy cavalry regiments was of 905 officers and men each; the only exception to this rule was the 1st Dragoons that had 1,083 officers and men (since it still comprised an additional troop).

Chapter 7

Light Dragoons and Hussars

During the first four decades of the 18th century, the heavy cavalry was the most important component of the European mounted troops, since it made up the bulk of the cavalry forces mobilised by the various nations and also because it had acquired a certain tactical supremacy on the battlefields of the continent. Highly trained and disciplined, it consisted of horsemen armed with long swords having a straight blade and mounted on massive horses. These could charge and manoeuvre in perfect order by maintaining knee-to-knee close formations. This kind of cavalry was mostly employed to conduct frontal charges and to cover the retreat of the line infantry when it was routed by the enemy. Following the Thirty Years' War, in fact, cavalry had started to perform a series of auxiliary roles for the infantry and was rarely used in an autonomous way.

Formations and battle tactics

At the beginning of the 18th century, the tactics and formations of the line infantry were extremely static: while moving on the battlefield, the line infantrymen advanced in columns; when stopping to open fire upon the enemy, they were deployed into long lines. After some rolling volleys of musketry were exchanged between two opposing infantry formations, a clash could continue in two different ways: on most occasions, one of the two lines was shattered by the enemy fire and thus retreated (at this point it was usually charged by the enemy cavalry); on some occasions, instead, it was fought hand-to-hand with bayonets. Keeping order in the formations and delivering a regular fire were the key factors behind victory; as a result, training was absolutely decisive to transform line infantry into an effective tactical tool. Generally, battles were extremely static, since maintaining perfect order in the formations obliged both the line infantrymen and the heavy cavalrymen to move slowly. The transition from the column formation to the line one was extremely delicate, since it exposed the fusiliers to the sudden charges of cavalry. When confronting cavalry, line infantry usually adopted a standard defensive formation known as 'square': this was another kind of close order, created with the aim of stopping enemy attacks by using the bayonets as pikes against mounted troops. The formations and tactics described were determined by the performances of the muskets that were used during the 18th century; these were flintlock weapons, with complicated loading operations. This meant that only one or two balls were shot in a minute, considering the standards of a line infantryman with good training. In addition, the flintlock muskets of this period were all smoothbores and extremely inaccurate: when a ball was fired, it came out from the weapon without a precise direction since there were no grooves inside the barrel to guide it. A flintlock musket was of some use only when fired at 100 or 200 metres from the target and as a result, during a battle, the line infantry formations had to be very close to the enemy in order to use their weapons effectively. The muskets of this age were also extremely heavy and this limited mobility of foot soldiers when traversing broken terrain such as that covered with rocks or with trees, and this meant it was practically impossible for them to keep the close formations in order. All the main tactical formations had been created for an 'ideal' battlefield, consisting of a large plain where the opposing infantries and cavalries could move without encountering obstacles. Heavy cavalry units made a very limited use of firearms. A couple of flintlock pistols were generally carried by each horseman, but these could be fired only from the short distance so were of little use. Dragoons, who were by now no longer mounted infantrymen, carried flintlock carbines, but these were generally used only when the soldiers dismounted to fight on foot. As we have discussed, in the military system of the early 18th century, soldiers were not required to think and act in an autonomous way: they only had to move as ordered in accordance with orders received. There was no space for initiative and each infraction of discipline was punished.

The drills required on the battlefield were repeated every day during training sessions, under the incessant beat of the drums. A perfect example of the kind of war fought in the 18th century was represented by the Prussian Army of Frederick the Great. He perfected close line infantry and heavy cavalry tactics to the maximum and was admired by all the officer corps of Europe. His soldiers were the best in the world and

Above left: Officer of the Light Dragoons wearing M1784 uniform. (ASKB)

Above right: Trooper of the Light Dragoons wearing M1784 uniform. (ASKB)

their methods of training were copied by all the armies whether enemy or ally. During the War of the Austrian Succession (1740–48) and the Seven Years' War (1756–63), however, some episodes showed that the Prussian heavy cavalry was not as perfect as it appeared. It became apparent, in fact, that it could experience serious problems while operating on broken terrain and when fighting against enemy units that employed hit-and-run guerrilla tactics. In particular, the Prussians had serious problems in countering the efficient light troops deployed by the Austrian Empire: these consisted of semi-regular light cavalrymen, recruited from the Balkans.

The light cavalrymen of the Austrian Army, commonly known as hussars, had been fighting for decades against the Ottoman Turks on the southern frontier of the Austrian Empire. The Turks lived in a state of endless conflict. During the conflict, both sides launched rapid incursions into the territory of the enemy to raid and pillage as much as possible. Gradually, the Austrian frontier soldiers learned to fight like their enemies, becoming expert in the art of skirmishing and scouting. Their usual area of operations was covered by mountains and woods, where each soldier had to move singularly and not in close formation. These fighters were the direct heirs of a glorious military tradition, which had originated in Hungary during the late Renaissance. The hussars were the Hungarian national cavalry in the same way that the uhlans (lancers) were the Polish national cavalry. Most of the light horsemen from Hungary were farmers during their civil lives and lived on the Balkan frontier as military settlers. As a result, their innovative tactics derived from direct combat experience and were based on the principle of open formation.

Open formation tactics

Each cavalryman was to advance in an autonomous way but always keep in contact with the other members of his unit; this way he could cover his advance behind the obstacles of the terrain (a tree, for example) and fire upon the enemy from a favourable position. With this kind of tactic, firearms were important for cavalry and could start playing a prominent role. During the War of the Austrian Succession, on several occasions, the Hungarian light cavalrymen of the Austrian Army caused serious trouble and losses to Frederick the Great's heavy mounted troops. The other great powers of Europe, unlike Austria, could not count on a militarised border from which expert light mounted fighters could be recruited; as a result, they started to create their own light cavalry corps by recruiting Hungarian mercenaries or prisoners of war. This was the case in France and of several other European nations, where hussar units proliferated during the central decades of the 18th century.

The new light horsemen of the European armies adopted the same uniforms and weapons as the Hungarian hussars, but very soon some local versions of it started to appear. In some countries, such as Great Britain, in fact, the new light cavalry assumed distinctive features and was quite different to that

Above left: **Officer of the Light Dragoons wearing M1796 uniform. (ASKB)**

Above right: **Officer of the Light Dragoons wearing M1796 uniform and M1812 shako. (ASKB)**

of Austria or France. The general expansion of these units continued well after the end of the War of the Austrian Succession, since the combat experiences of the following Seven Years' War confirmed the tactical importance of the new light corps. A new form of warfare was born: the 'petite guerre' or 'little war', which was based on low-intensity combat and hit-and-run tactics.

The British Army was greatly affected by the light cavalry revolution that took place in the 18th century. Its cavalry, in fact, was completely reorganised and modernised during the crucial years that saw the end of the War of the Austrian Succession and the outbreak of the Jacobite rising (1745–48). It should be noted, however, that in Britain the introduction of new light cavalry tactics encountered very strong opposition: the British officer corps of the time, especially that of cavalry, was an extremely conservative one that considered as suspicious any innovation coming from abroad. In time, however, evidence obliged the traditionalists to abandon their positions.

Reorganising the British Army

Until 1745, the British Army comprised only heavy cavalry units (horse regiments) and medium cavalry units (dragoon regiments). In that year, however, the Jacobite rising began in Scotland. In response, the British mounted units experienced some difficulties in chasing up the highly mobile insurgent forces of Highlanders, who moved very rapidly on the broken terrain of the Highlands and who were masters of hit-and-run tactics. As a result, the Duke of Kingston, an English noble who supported the British military efforts against the Jacobites, raised a volunteer horse regiment having light cavalry training from his land possessions in Nottinghamshire. This new corps, organised by the Duke at his own expense, was officially ranked as the 10th Regiment of Horse of the British Army but its members were trained as light cavalrymen despite being equipped and attired like standard heavy horsemen. The Duke of Kingston's Regiment of Horse performed extremely well during the Jacobite rising and participated in the decisive Battle of Culloden, after which it pursued the defeated Jacobites with great determination.

After the end of the Jacobite rising, in 1746, the experimental volunteer regiment raised by the Duke of Kingston was disbanded; its members, in fact, had enlisted only for the duration of the war. The Duke of Cumberland, who had commanded the British Army during the Battle of Culloden, had a very positive opinion of the unit and wished to retain it in service. This was not possible for practical reasons, but the Duke found a way to maintain some light cavalry in his military forces. He organised a new light cavalry unit, known as the Duke of Cumberland's Regiment of Light Dragoons, in which he enlisted all the men of the recently disbanded Duke of Kingston's Regiment of Horse. The new corps was the first regular light cavalry unit ever formed in the British Army and was the first to be ranked as Light Dragoons. The regiment was soon dispatched to continental Europe and participated in the final operations of the War of the Austrian Succession, distinguishing itself at the Battle of Lauffeld. In 1749, however, the Duke of Cumberland's Regiment of Light Dragoons was disbanded following the cessation of hostilities in Europe.

The Duke of Cumberland was one of the first British military officers to understand the importance and the potential of the new light cavalry corps; during the Jacobite rising, for example, he had a small personal bodyguard formed by a few hussars who were recruited in Hungary. Despite being just a few men, they fought with distinction at the Battle of Culloden and gave a good impression of themselves to the officers of the British Army. These Duke of Cumberland's Hussars were the first unit of the British Army to wear the traditional dress of the Hungarian light cavalry. Until 1757, the British cavalry forces continued to be made up of horse and dragoon regiments, since the experimental cavalry corps active during 1745–49 were all disbanded with the end of the ongoing wars. It was just a question of time, however, before Britain was to be involved in a new conflict. Some years later, in fact, the Seven Years'

War broke out and the British Army was involved in a new large-scale European war. The need for new light cavalry units became increasingly strong in all the major armies of the time. In April 1757, the formation of a total of 11 independent troops of light cavalry was authorised.

Light cavalry

Each was attached to one of the existing horse regiments and had the following internal establishment: three officers, one troop quartermaster, five NCOs, two drummers and 60 troopers.

Members of these new troops were chosen from the youngest and fittest recruits of the existing horse regiments; they were mounted on small and nimble horses, being trained to act as skirmishers and explorers. The new light horsemen continued to wear the standard uniforms of their parent regiments but received distinctive headgear. This was a black leather helmet with an upright comb, a frontal plate mounted with brass and a drooping feather. They were still armed with swords having straight blade, but also carried a flintlock carbine and a couple of pistols. The tradition of the British Light Dragoons was

Above left: Trooper of the 13th Light Dragoons wearing M1812 uniform. (ASKB)

Above right: Trooper of the 13th Light Dragoons wearing M1812 uniform.

born: in a few years, in fact, the new light troops proved their potential so that in 1759 it was decided to form seven completely independent regiments of light cavalry.

The light cavalry regiments recruited very rapidly and were numbered in progressive order after the 14 regiments of dragoons that existed at the time. The following new units of Light Dragoons were organised:

15th Regiment of Light Dragoons

It was raised in the London area by British Army Officer George Augustus Eliott (1717–90) and distinguished itself during the Battle of Emsdorf (1760) fought in Germany. After taking part in the Battle of Wilhelmsthal it returned home. During 1766–69, there was an attempt to give a separate numeration to the regiments of Light Dragoons and thus the unit became the 1st Regiment of Light Dragoons. When this experiment ended, the corps received its original denomination.

16th Regiment of Light Dragoons

This unit, raised by British General John Burgoyne (1722–92), took part in the final operations of the Seven Years' War. During 1766–69, it was named as the 2nd Regiment of Light Dragoons.

17th Regiment of Light Dragoons

Raised in Scotland, it was disbanded at the end of the Seven Years' War.

18th Regiment of Light Dragoons

This unit saw some action in Germany during 1761 and was renamed as the 3rd Regiment of Light Dragoons in 1766. During 1769, it was ranked as the 17th Regiment of Light Dragoons since the unit originally having that denomination had been disbanded.

19th Regiment of Light Dragoons

Renamed as the 4th Regiment of Light Dragoons in 1766. During 1769, it was ranked as the 18th Regiment of Light Dragoons. It was formed by brigading some of the light troops that had been created in 1757.

20th Regiment of Light Dragoons

Raised in Ireland and then disbanded at the end of the Seven Years' War, it was formed by brigading some of the light troops that had been created in 1757.

21st Regiment of Light Dragoons

Raised in England, it was disbanded at the end of the Seven Years' War. It was formed by brigading some of the light troops that had been created in 1757.

By 1765, the British cavalry comprised a total of four regiments of Light Dragoons, which were

Troopers (left) and officers (right) of the light dragoons from the King's German Legion.

augmented to five in 1768 when the 12th Regiment of Dragoons was transformed into the 12th Regiment of Light Dragoons. The combat experiences of the Seven Years' War had shown the importance of having good light cavalry and thus, when the American Revolution began, the British government expanded its own mounted troops by adding more light cavalry corps:

19th Regiment of Light Dragoons
Raised in 1779, it was disbanded in 1783.

20th Regiment of Light Dragoons
Raised in 1779, it was disbanded in 1783.

21st Regiment of Light Dragoons
Raised in 1779, it was disbanded in 1783.

22nd Regiment of Light Dragoons
Raised in 1779, it was disbanded in 1783.

23rd Regiment of Light Dragoons
Raised in 1781.

Most of these new units were temporary corps with a very short history; the only exception was the 23rd Regiment, which became the new 19th Light Dragoons when the corps originally given the name was disbanded in 1783. In any case, the British light cavalry distinguished itself in North America and clearly showed its superiority when confronted with the mounted troops deployed by the Thirteen Colonies. The broken terrain of North America did not permit the use of large cavalry contingents and limited the movements of all the mounted soldiers having heavy personal equipment; as a result, the Light Dragoons were the only horse soldiers that could operate in an effective way in that theatre of operations. Of the light cavalry units that were part of the British Army during 1775–83, only two, the 16th Light Dragoons and the 17th Light Dragoons, served in North America and thus could learn something from the combat experiences of the American Revolution.

In addition to the creation of the new short-lived units listed above, the years of the American Revolution also saw the transformation of several existing heavy cavalry corps into regiments of Light Dragoons:

- The 7th Regiment of Dragoons became the 7th Regiment of Light Dragoons in 1783
- The 8th Regiment of Dragoons became the 8th Regiment of Light Dragoons in 1776
- The 9th Regiment of Dragoons became the 9th Regiment of Light Dragoons in 1783
- The 10th Regiment of Dragoons became the 10th Regiment of Light Dragoons in 1783
- The 11th Regiment of Dragoons became the 11th Regiment of Light Dragoons in 1783
- The 13th Regiment of Dragoons became the 13th Regiment of Light Dragoons in 1783
- The 14th Regiment of Dragoons became the 14th Regiment of Light Dragoons in 1776

By 1785, the British cavalry comprised 13 light units (numbered 7–19, in progressive order after the six existing regiments of dragoons). With the outbreak of the Revolutionary Wars, the expansion of the British light cavalry continued with the creation of the following units (many of which were short-lived):

- 20th Regiment of Light Dragoons: raised in 1792, disbanded in 1818
- 21st Regiment of Light Dragoons: raised in 1794, disbanded in 1819
- 22nd, 23rd and 24th Regiment of Light Dragoons: raised in 1794, disbanded in 1802
- 25th Regiment of Light Dragoons: raised in 1794. It later became the 22nd Light Dragoons and was disbanded in 1820
- 26th Regiment of Light Dragoons: raised in 1794. It later became the 23rd Light Dragoons and was disbanded in 1817
- 27th Regiment of Light Dragoons: raised in 1794. It later became the 24th Light Dragoons and was disbanded in 1819
- 28th Regiment of Light Dragoons: raised in 1794, disbanded in 1802
- 29th Regiment of Light Dragoons: raised in 1794. It later became the 25th Light Dragoons and was disbanded in 1819
- 30th, 31st, 32nd and 33rd Regiment of Light Dragoons: raised in 1794, disbanded in 1796

In 1803, the British cavalry included a total of 19 regiments of Light Dragoons. They formed the bulk of the British mounted troops and were sent to fight overseas much more frequently than the heavy cavalry regiments. Thanks to their tactical flexibility, they could be used to perform a variety of different tasks and could operate on any kind of terrain.

During the early years of the Napoleonic Wars, the French hussars obtained a series of brilliant victories and became famous for their incredible courage as well as for their ornate uniforms. The British Army also fell victim to the French vogue for hussars and thus during 1806–07 some of its Light Dragoon regiments were transformed into hussar ones. In total, four units were involved into this conversion: the 7th, 10th, 15th Light and 18th Light Dragoons. The transformation of these units into Hussar regiments did not affect their training and tactical functions; it did not change their progressive number but simply saw the introduction of new and much more costly uniforms. Shortly after the Battle of Waterloo, during which the British officers were impressed by the combat capabilities of the French lancers, three regiments of Light Dragoons (the 9th, 12th and 16th) were transformed into lancer units.

The British Light Dragoons did not improve their combat capabilities in a significant way during 1770–92. By the outbreak of the Revolutionary Wars, in fact, they were used to operate in the same way as the rest of the British cavalry and had retained very little of their original 'light' nature. To address this problem and to improve the general quality of the light mounted units, as early as 1778 a *Discipline of the Light Horse* was published by Captain Hinde. The publication contained detailed information regarding the training and equipment of the light horsemen but, unfortunately for the British Light Dragoons, it was not well read and never put into practice. At Wellington's orders,

Officer of the 15th Hussars. (ASKB)

especially in the Iberian Peninsula, the British light mounted troops would have learned most from experience.

7th Regiment of Light Dragoons

Raised in 1690 as part of the Scots Army, during an expansion period ordered by William of Orange after the Glorious Revolution. As a dragoon regiment, it participated in the Grand Alliance War and in the War of the Spanish Succession in continental Europe. Later it fought in the Jacobite rising of 1715, taking part in the Battle of Sheriffmuir. During the War of the Austrian Succession, it participated in the battles of Dettingen, Fontenoy, Rocoux and Lauffeld. In 1760, it took part in the Battle of Warburg during the Seven Years' War. In 1783, the unit was converted into a regiment of Light Dragoons and as such it was sent to Flanders to fight against Revolutionary France. In 1807, it was transformed into a hussar unit. During the following year, it was sent to the Iberian Peninsula to fight at Sir John Moore's orders. After the end of that unlucky campaign, which saw the French invasion of Portugal, the 7th Hussars remained in Britain until 1813 when it returned to the Iberian Peninsula. It participated in the Battle of Orthes in southern France before being despatched home in 1814. When Napoleon returned from his exile, the regiment took part with distinction in the Belgian Campaign and to the Battle of Waterloo.

8th Regiment of Light Dragoons

Raised during 1693 in Ireland, as a dragoon unit it participated in the War of the Spanish Succession suffering heavy losses. After being completely reorganised, it took part in the crushing of the Jacobite rising. The corps returned to Scotland when the Jacobite rising of 1745 began and in 1776 it was transformed into a regiment of Light Dragoons. As such it took part in the Flanders Campaign fought against Revolutionary France, before being despatched to India in 1802 where it took part in several important military actions against the Marathas and the Gurkhas. The unit returned to Europe in 1819, after having been converted into a hussar corps.

9th Regiment of Light Dragoons

This unit was created during the Jacobite rising of 1715, as part of the British military response to the Scottish revolt. After many years spent in Ireland performing garrison duties, it ceased to be a regiment of dragoons and was converted into a unit of Light Dragoons (1783). During 1798, the corps participated with distinction in the suppression of the Irish Revolt. In 1806–07, it took part in the disastrous British military expedition directed against the Spanish colonies of South America (Argentina and Uruguay). In 1809, it participated in the unlucky Walcheren Campaign. The unit was later sent to the Iberian Peninsula, where it took part in several actions during 1811–12. In 1813, it returned to Britain and performed garrison duties until the end of the Napoleonic Wars; in 1816 the corps was transformed into a regiment of lancers.

10th Regiment of Light Dragoons

This unit was created during the Jacobite rising of 1715, as part of the British military response to the Scottish revolt. For 25 years it remained of garrison in Cornwall until being despatched to Scotland in 1745 to fight against the Jacobites. During the Seven Years' War, it was sent to continental Europe, participating with distinction in the clashes of Minden and Warburg. In 1783, the corps was transformed into a regiment of Light Dragoons but did not take part in any military campaigns until being converted into a hussar unit in 1807. During the following year, it was sent to the Iberian Peninsula, where it fought at Sir John Moore's orders. Before returning to Britain, it participated with distinction in the

Battle of Benavente (1808) during which it captured the commander of the French cavalry, General Lefebvre-Desnouettes (1773–1822). In 1813, the regiment was sent again to the Iberian Peninsula and during the following year, it participated in Wellington's invasion of southern France. In 1815, it was part of the British military forces that were deployed to Belgium and charged against the French at Waterloo.

11th Regiment of Light Dragoons

This regiment was also created as a dragoon unit during the Jacobite rising of 1715. It remained a garrison in Scotland for several years and participated in the crushing of the 1745 Jacobite Rising. In 1760, the corps was despatched to Germany in order to take part in the Seven Years' War; during that same year it fought at the Battle of Warburg. In 1783, together with several other regiments, the unit was transformed into a corps of Light Dragoons. Small detachments of the 11th Light Dragoons participated in the Flanders Campaign and in the later Anglo-Russian invasion of Holland (1799). In 1801, the unit was deployed for a brief period in Egypt, before remaining as a garrison at home for several years. During 1811, it was sent to the Iberian Peninsula, where it fought at Badajoz and Salamanca (1812) before returning to Britain. In 1815, it took part in the Belgian Campaign and the Battle of Waterloo.

12th Regiment of Light Dragoons

This regiment was formed as a dragoon unit during the Jacobite rising of 1715. Three years later, it was placed on the Irish establishment of the British Army and was sent to Ireland to act as a garrison unit. It operated as such for 75 years, being transformed into a regiment of Light Dragoons in 1768. During 1794, the unit finally saw some action, and took part in the attack against the French defences of Bastia (in Corsica). In 1801, the regiment was sent to Egypt where it participated in the Battle of Alexandria. After a few years spent in Britain, in 1809 it was made part of the British expeditionary force that landed at Walcheren in the Netherlands. During 1811–14, the 12th Light Dragoons were, at Wellington's orders, in the Iberian Peninsula, distinguishing themselves at the Battle of Salamanca. After a brief period spent in Britain, the regiment was sent to Belgium in 1815 and fought with determination at Waterloo. Soon after the end of the hostilities, it was transformed into a unit of lancers.

Trooper of the 15th Hussars.

13th Regiment of Light Dragoons

Raised during the military emergency caused by the Jacobite Rebellion of 1715, it was later despatched to Ireland where it remained as garrison until 1742. With the outbreak of the 1745 Jacobite rising, it was sent to Scotland, where it suffered heavy casualties during a series of minor clashes that were fought against the rebel Highlanders. After the end of the revolt, the unit was returned to Ireland, where it was transformed into a regiment of Light Dragoons in 1783. A small detachment of the corps served in the West Indies during 1795–98, but the unit did not see any major fighting for several years. In 1810, it was despatched to the Iberian Peninsula, where it served with distinction until 1814. After taking part in the invasion of southern France, the regiment was briefly sent home; in 1815, with the return of Napoleon, it fought at Waterloo. During that clash, the 13th Light Dragoons conducted several charges against the enemy and suffered significant losses.

14th Regiment of Light Dragoons

Raised during the military emergency caused by the Jacobite Rebellion of 1715, it was later despatched to Ireland where it remained as garrison until 1742. With the outbreak of the 1745 Jacobite rising, it was sent to Scotland, where it suffered heavy casualties during a series of minor clashes that were fought against the rebel Highlanders. After the end of the revolt, the unit returned to Ireland, where it was transformed into a regiment of Light Dragoons in 1776. Two of the unit's troops participated in the Flanders Campaign, while seven were sent to the West Indies in 1795 to support the Haitian Revolution against the French. In 1808, the 14th Light Dragoons were sent to the Iberian Peninsula, where they remained until 1814. The regiment soon demonstrated that it was one of the best cavalry corps of the British Army, since it took part with distinction in several important clashes such as those of Salamanca and Vittoria. In the summer of 1814, after participating in the invasion of southern France, the unit returned to Britain for some months. Very soon, however, two of its squadrons were despatched to North America when the ongoing conflict between Great Britain and North America entered its final stage. The detachment of the 14th Light Dragoons fought at the bloody Battle of New Orleans in 1815, which was one of the worst defeats suffered by the British Army during the Napoleonic Period.

Trooper of the 15th Hussars. (ASKB)

15th Regiment of Light Dragoons

Created as a Light Dragoon regiment in 1759, the unit was soon sent to continental Europe in order to participate to the Seven Years' War. It distinguished itself during the Battle of Emsdorf and took part in the Battle of Wilhelmsthal before returning home. In 1793, it was sent to Flanders, where it fought against the French on several occasions. During 1799, the corps was made part of the British expeditionary force that participated in the unlucky Anglo-Russian invasion of Holland. In 1807, the unit was converted into a hussar corps and as such, in 1808, it was sent to the Iberian Peninsula. During the following year, the 15th Light Dragoons returned home, but in 1813 they were sent back to Spain. They participated in the decisive Battle of Vittoria and in the ensuing invasion of southern France (fighting at Orthez and

Toulouse). In 1815, the corps took part in the Belgian Campaign and was present at Waterloo. A few years after the end of the Napoleonic Wars, in 1819, this regiment charged against the protesting crowd during the so-called 'Peterloo Massacre'.

16th Regiment of Light Dragoons

Formed as a Light Dragoon regiment in 1759, it participated in the Seven Years' War and was sent to Portugal to support the country's military efforts against Spain. In 1776, it was despatched to the Thirteen Colonies in order to crush the American Revolution where it took part in several important engagements: Brandywine (1777), Germantown (1777) and Monmouth (1778). During 1779, it returned to Britain. With the outbreak of the Revolutionary Wars, the 16th Light Dragoons was despatched to Flanders. Here it took part in several engagements before returning home in 1796. After a period spent performing garrison duties in Ireland, the regiment was despatched to the Iberian Peninsula in 1809. In Spain, the soldiers of the corps distinguishing themselves at several engagements: Talavera, Bussaco (1810), Salamanca and Vittoria. With the return of Napoleon from his exile, the unit participated in the Belgian Campaign of 1815 and in the Battle of Waterloo.

17th Regiment of Light Dragoons

Raised as a Light Dragoon regiment in 1759, it was sent to North America in 1775 and was the only cavalry unit of the British Army that participated in the military operations of the entire American Revolution. A detachment from the regiment, in 1777, was used to create the famous British legion commanded by British general Banastre Tarleton (1754–1833); which fought with counter-guerrilla methods against the American insurgents and obtained a series of minor victories during the central years of the American Revolution. Following the end of hostilities in North America, the 17th Light Dragoons returned home and were assigned to the garrison of Ireland. In 1795, two of its troops were sent to the West Indies to crush local revolts. During 1806–07, the regiment took part in the disastrous British military expedition directed against the Spanish colonies of South America (present day Argentina and Uruguay). In 1808, the corps was sent to India, where it remained until the end of the Napoleonic Wars.

18th Regiment of Light Dragoons

Organised as a Light Dragoon regiment in 1759, during 1796–97 it was sent to the West Indies to fight the French. In 1799, it took part in the unlucky Anglo-Russian invasion of Holland, during which it fought at the Battle of Bergen. In 1808, the unit was despatched to the Iberian Peninsula after having been converted into a hussar corps the previous year. In 1809, the 18th Light Dragoons returned to Britain but in 1813 they were sent back to Spain; here, at Wellington's orders, they participated in the Battle of Vittoria. In 1814, the unit spent some months at home, before being sent to Belgium when Napoleon returned to France. It took part in the Battle of Waterloo, during which it charged against the French.

19th Regiment of Light Dragoons

This unit was created during 1781 specifically for service in India. At that time, the British Empire did not have any European cavalry corps in the Indian sub-continent and the regiment was the first unit of the regular British cavalry to serve in India. It participated with distinction in both the Anglo-Mysore Wars and the Anglo-Maratha Wars, before fighting at the decisive Battle of Assaye (1803) under the command of a young Wellington. In 1806, the 19th Light Dragoons returned to Britain and performed garrison duties until the outbreak of hostilities between Britain and the America, where they were sent in 1812. They remained until 1816, being the only cavalry unit of the British Army that participated in the military operations of the entire war of 1812. The regiment fought with great professionalism in North

America, acting as the main cavalry unit of the British Army in that part of the world. In 1816, it was re-equipped as a corps of lancers.

20th Regiment of Light Dragoons

Raised in 1792, this unit was created specifically for service in Jamaica. Its main task was to counter the activities of the maroons who attacked the British plantations on the rich island of the West Indies. In 1807, after many years of service in Jamaica, the corps took part in the disastrous British military expedition directed against the Spanish colonies of South America (Argentina and Uruguay). During that same year, one squadron of the regiment participated in the so-called Alexandria Expedition, a punitive raid directed against Ottoman Egypt and one of Britain's lesser known military operations of the Napoleonic Wars. In 1808, the 20th Light Dragoons were sent to the Iberian Peninsula, where it fought at the Battle of Vimeiro before returning home. The unit was disbanded in 1818, during the great demobilisation that took place following the end of the Napoleonic Period.

Officer of the 18th Hussars.

21st Regiment of Light Dragoons

Raised in 1794 and being commonly known as the Yorkshire Light Dragoons, this was a very short-lived corps that was disbanded in 1819 after having spent the entire period of the Napoleonic Wars in Ireland.

22nd Regiment of Light Dragoons

Raised in 1794 for service in India, this unit took part in the British occupation of Java during 1811 and remained garrison on the island until 1813. After the annexation of the Netherlands to the French Empire in 1811, the British government occupied the Dutch colonial territories of present day Indonesia in order to prevent the French from obtaining direct control over the territories. Java, the most important of the Dutch colonial possessions, was invaded in 1811 by a British expeditionary force organised in India. The island was returned to the Netherlands only at the end of the Napoleonic Wars. In 1820, the 22nd Regiment of Light Dragoons was disbanded.

23rd Regiment of Light Dragoons

Raised in 1794, this unit served with great distinction during the Napoleonic Period. Its first major deployment overseas was in Egypt, where the British and the Ottomans fought against the French until obtaining a complete victory in 1801. With the outbreak of the Peninsular War, the corps was sent to Spain, where it participated in several engagements and fought with great determination at the Battle of Talavera. After a brief period spent in Britain, the 23rd Light Dragoons took part in the Belgian Campaign of 1815 and the Battle of Waterloo. The regiment was disbanded in 1817.

24th Regiment of Light Dragoons

Raised in 1794 for service in India, this unit participated in the Second Anglo-Maratha War (1803–05) and didn't return to Britain until it was disbanded in 1819.

25th Regiment of Light Dragoons

Raised in 1794 for service in India, this unit participated in the Second Anglo-Maratha War and only returned to Britain when disbanded in 1819. In 1810, one of the troops from this regiment took part in the British occupation of Mauritius (a French colony at that time).

26th, 27th, 28th and 29th Regiment of Light Dragoons

This was one of the eight regiments of Light Dragoons raised in 1794 as part of the great mobilisation that took place after the outbreak of hostilities with Revolutionary France. It was disbanded in 1802 following the Peace of Amiens, without having seen action.

30th, 31st, 32nd, 33rd Regiment of Light Dragoons

This was one of the eight regiments of Light Dragoons raised in 1794 as part of the great mobilisation that took place after the outbreak of hostilities with Revolutionary France. It was disbanded in 1796 following the end of Flanders Campaign, without having seen action.

The internal organisation of the regiments of Light Dragoons changed very little during the Napoleonic Period. They were structured with ten troops each, with two troops making up a squadron. Squadrons were known by numbers, troops were known by letters (it was the opposite for the heavy cavalry regiments). Of the five squadrons, one was a depot

Officer of the 18th Hussars. (ASKB)

unit that was always kept in reserve in Britain and was never sent to serve overseas. The depot squadron of each regiment had to provide new recruits with solid basic training to the four active squadrons in order to replenish the losses suffered during overseas deployments. In 1813, two additional troops were added to each regiment of Light Dragoons, in order to form a fifth active squadron.

The regimental staff of the light cavalry units comprised the following elements: one colonel, two lieutenant-colonels, two majors, six captains, one captain-lieutenant, eight lieutenants, nine cornets, one paymaster, one adjutant, one surgeon, two assistant-surgeons and one veterinary surgeon.

Each troop, instead, included the following: one captain, one lieutenant-colonel, one major, one quartermaster, four sergeants, four corporals, one trumpeter and 90 troopers. In June 1809, the quartermaster of each troop was transformed into a sergeant-major and a lieutenant-quartermaster was added to the staff of each regiment.

During 1810, the internal composition of a light cavalry unit's regimental staff was partly modified and became the following one: one colonel, one lieutenant-colonel, one major, one adjutant, one lieutenant-quartermaster, one paymaster, one surgeon, two assistant-surgeons, one veterinary surgeon and one regimental sergeant-major.

The new composition of a single troop, instead, was this: one captain, one lieutenant, one cornet, one troop sergeant-major, three sergeants, four corporals, one trumpeter, one farrier and 63 troopers. By 1809, the average numerical consistency of most light cavalry regiments was of 905 officers and men each. The units transformed into hussar corps retained their previous internal organisation.

Above left: Trooper of the hussars from the King's German Legion.

Above right: Hussars from the King's German Legion in 1815.

Chapter 8
Artillery and Specialist Corps

Gunner of the foot artillery wearing pre-1797 uniform. (ASKB)

U ntil the beginning of the 18th century, the artillerymen of most of the European armies were required to fire their guns but were not equipped to defend themselves from enemy attacks. As a result, while on the battlefield, they had to be escorted by infantrymen specifically charged to do so. Until 1716, with the creation of the Royal Artillery, the British Army did not comprise any permanent company or battery of artillery. Temporary artillery trains were organised by the Ordnance Department only when needed and were usually disbanded at the end of each campaign.

In time of peace, dozens of professional gunners were at the service of the Ordnance Department; they were scattered across Britain and manned the guns of the various garrisons. In case of war, they were assembled to form a train and were supplemented with the needed number of civilian mattrosses and pioneers, the latter being semi-skilled civilian labourers who were contracted only for the duration of a campaign. The conductors of the carts used to move the artillery pieces were all civilians. As a result, the 18th century was a period of great change and of progressive professionalisation for the British artillery and for the smaller technical corps that supported it. The first two permanent companies/batteries of artillery of the British Army were organised in 1716, and were structured as independent corps. In 1720, they received the official denomination Royal Artillery, but in practice they were an autonomous military force. Before long the two original companies were increased to four and were assembled – at least from an administrative point of view – with the artillery companies that were the garrison in Gibraltar and Menorca since the end of the War of the Spanish Succession. As a result of these organisational changes, in 1722 Royal Regiment of Artillery was created.

The new regiment had the numerical consistency of a single battalion, and before long its members were famed for their great personal preparation and professionalism. From its start, in fact, selection and promotion in the Royal Artillery were based on merit.

In 1741, in order to improve the general quality of all the artillerymen serving across the British Empire, a cadet company was formed at the Royal Military Academy of Woolwich; this was tasked with training the officers of the Royal Artillery Regiment and also those artillery officers who were at the service of the British East India Company. In

Above left: Gunner of the foot artillery wearing M1797 uniform with bicorn. (ASKB)

Above middle: Officer of the foot artillery wearing M1797 uniform. (ASKB)

Above right: Gunner of the foot artillery wearing M1797 uniform with M1800 shako. (ASKB)

1757, the Royal Artillery Regiment was reorganised into two battalions with 12 companies each, but its expansion continued during the following decades.

By 1780, it comprised the following sub-units: four active battalions with eight companies each, two 'invalid' independent companies employed to perform garrison duties, and a permanent military band.

By 1803, the year during which the hostilities with France resumed, the Royal Artillery consisted of eight battalions with ten companies/batteries each; a 9th Battalion was raised in 1806 and a 10th Battalion was formed in 1808. The various battalions were not employed on the field as complete units, since their companies/batteries were usually deployed as autonomous corps. When this happened, they were commonly known as brigades despite consisting of companies with just six pieces each. Attached to each brigade was a detachment of artillery drivers, tasked with moving the guns on the field.

The standard establishment of a Royal Artillery's company/battery/brigade comprised the following elements: two captains, two first-lieutenants, one second-lieutenant, four sergeants, four corporals, nine bombardiers, three drummers and 116 gunners. Of the six artillery pieces that were manned by a company/battery/brigade, on most occasions five were field guns and one was a howitzer. These were transported together with their limbers and with some wagons that were essential for their correct functioning: eight ammunition-wagons, three baggage-wagons and one spare-wheel wagon. In addition, each artillery brigade also had a field forge that was fundamental for repairing damaged pieces. A total of about 100 drivers and 200 draught animals were usually needed to move a single artillery battery. Generally, the traditional foot artillery moved very slowly on the battlefields of the early 19th century and changed position rarely during a field battle.

Horse-drawn artillery

To have greater capacity than the reach of the foot artillery, during the Seven Years' War the Prussian monarch Frederick the Great developed a new form of artillery capable of moving much more rapidly on the battlefields using lighter guns drawn by horses. Initially Frederick's idea appeared too innovative for its time; however, it became clear that the new horse-drawn artillery could have an enormous tactical potential. Horse batteries could be deployed very easily to the points of the battlefield where their presence was needed. In addition, they could support the attacks launched by the cavalry since they could move at the same pace as the horsemen. Obviously, creating a new branch of service was not simple: new and lighter guns, specifically designed for the horse batteries, had to be created. In addition, the artillerymen and the horses of the new mounted batteries had to undergo training.

Officer of the foot artillery wearing M1812 uniform. (ASKB)

By the outbreak of the French Revolution, horse artillery was already a stable presence in most of the major European armies. Prussia, for example, had three companies of horse artillery in 1792. Several other nations followed suit during the last decades of the 18th century and organised their own units of mounted artillery: Austria (1778), Hanover (1786), Denmark-Norway (1790), France (1791) and Sweden (1792).

New horse-drawn carriages were developed and specific tactics for the employment of mounted artillery were formulated. The British Army organised two troops of this new branch during January 1793. Unlike the foot artillery, the batteries of the horse artillery were known as troops and not as companies. The internal organisation of the new mounted batteries remained similar to those of the cavalry troops, and this was apparent in the uniforms used by the horse artillerymen that were of 'light cavalry' cut. In November 1793, another two troops of horse artillery were organised and these, together with the two existing ones, showed their great tactical flexibility during the Flanders Campaign. Each mounted battery was equipped with six 6-pounder horse-drawn guns. By 1801, the number of horse batteries in the British Army had been increased to seven, but continued to be expanded during the following years. By 1806, there were 12 troops of mounted artillery (and they were retained until the end of the Napoleonic Wars).

Each single troop of horse artillery comprised the following elements: one captain, one second-captain, three lieutenants, two staff sergeants, three sergeants, three corporals, six bombardiers, 80 gunners, 60 drivers, one farrier, one carriage-smith, two shoeing-smiths, two collar-makers, one wheel-wright and one trumpeter.

As in the foot artillery companies, the bombardiers by now did not have any specific duty as it had been during the previous centuries and their rank corresponded to that of lance-corporal. The gunners

Above left: Officer from the artillery of the King's German Legion wearing M1812 uniform.
(Photo and © Kings German Legion Artillery)

Above middle: NCO from the artillery of the King's German Legion wearing M1812 uniform.
(Photo and © Kings German Legion Artillery)

Above right: Gunner of the foot artillery wearing M1812 uniform. (ASKB)

were mounted on horses, while the drivers sat on the carriages or limbers of the guns when their battery moved. Each horse battery was divided into three divisions with two guns each. Each division had a subdivision with one gun each. A single division was commanded by a lieutenant, while a single subdivision was commanded by a sergeant or by a corporal. A single troop could also be divided into two half-brigades with three guns each, commanded by the captain or by the second-captain. Unlike the foot brigades, which were commonly known by the name of their commander, the horse batteries were known by letters. During the Napoleonic Wars, some detachments of the Royal Artillery started to be equipped with rockets instead of guns. At the beginning, these new weapons were not very popular in the British Army, until their effectivity became apparent. In India, in particular, the Royal Artillery employed rockets against the military forces of the local native rulers and obtained a series of memorable victories due to the psychological impact that the new weapons had on the enemy.

Above left: Gunner from the artillery of the King's German Legion wearing M1812 uniform.
(Photo and © Kings German Legion Artillery)

Above right: NCO (left) and gunner (right) from the artillery of the King's German Legion wearing fatigue dress.
(Photo and © Kings German Legion Artillery)

Above left: Trooper of the horse artillery wearing M1793 uniform. (ASKB)

Above middle: Officer of the horse artillery wearing M1799 uniform. (ASKB)

Above right: Trooper of the horse artillery wearing M1799 uniform.

Left: Trooper of the Rocket Troops (left) and trooper of the horse artillery (right) in 1815.

In 1813, two independent units of horse artillery armed with rockets were formed; these were commonly known as Rocket Troops and their members were dressed in a similar way to the standard horse artillerymen. A single troop equipped with rockets consisted of 172 soldiers and could carry 840 'missiles', so consequently had considerable firepower. The Rocket Troops, with their 'experimental' nature, participated in several engagements during 1814–15.

In 1793, the British Army militarised its artillery drivers. Up to that point, drivers were unreliable civilian contractors lacking military discipline and training. As a result, the new Corps of Royal Artillery Drivers was formed. It comprised soldiers, draught animals and the wagons that were needed to transport the weaponry. By 1808, the Corps of Royal Artillery Drivers, whose members dressed in a similar uniform to the soldiers of the horse artillery, comprised a total of eight troops. Each deployed 450 drivers organised into five sections of 90 men, 104 assorted craftsmen, 945 draught horses and 75 riding horses. Each troop was commanded by a captain.

By the end of the Napoleonic Wars, the Corps of Royal Artillery Drivers had been expanded to 11 troops, for a total of 88 officers and 7,352 other ranks. The sections of the artillery drivers' troops were divided among the artillery companies, with one section often attached to each battery. Wellington was never particularly happy with his Corps of Royal Artillery Drivers, because its members sometimes lacked discipline and were not guided by expert officers; as a result, in 1817, the Corps of Royal Artillery Drivers was temporarily absorbed into the Royal Artillery before being disbanded in 1822.

Corps of Royal Engineers

The Corps of Royal Engineers, like the Royal Artillery, was organised as a stable military unit in 1716. Until that time, the British Army had included only a few independent officers with specific engineering skills. The formation of an independent Corps of Engineers (the Royal prefix was added in 1787), however, did not change the existing situation in a significant way. Until the outbreak of the Napoleonic Wars, the British Engineers comprised a few commissioned officers who had undergone specific technical training at Woolwich. In 1792, there were 73 engineers, a number that was progressively augmented so that by 1813 the Corps of Royal Engineers mustered a total of 262 officers. The officers received higher pay when serving overseas and were consulted only when strictly needed, for example to conduct siege operations or to build military infrastructures such as bridges. The labour force for the Royal Engineers was provided by the Royal Military Artificers (known as Royal Military Artificers and Labourers until 1798). This small technical corps consisted of 12 companies of military workers, each commanded by a sub-lieutenant and by a staff sergeant. The Royal Military Artificers performed auxiliary tasks that were fundamental to the life of the British Army on the field, and included building and carpentry.

During the Napoleonic Wars, the 12 companies of this corps were scattered across the British Empire as follows: eight in Britain, two in Gibraltar, one in the West Indies and one in Canada (Nova Scotia).

The artificers of the British Army were organised as an independent military branch of service in 1772. In 1787, the corps was expanded and assumed the new official denomination of Royal Military Artificers and Labourers. During the first phase of the Napoleonic Wars, the corps mostly served in small detachments, since their companies were usually broken up and dispersed on different fronts. Wellington was never particularly happy with his artificers and in 1812, set about reorganising them. They assumed the new official denomination of Royal Sappers and Miners and their number expanded to 2,800 men. They were now commanded by the commissioned officers of the Royal Engineers. In addition, they no longer served in small detachments but in companies.

After being retrained in Britain, 300 workers of the Royal Sappers and Miners served with distinction in the Iberian Peninsula during 1813. Later, in 1815, they made a significant contribution to the British military effort that culminated in the Battle of Waterloo. During the Belgian Campaign, each division of Wellington's army had an attached brigade (company) of sappers and miners. The single companies transported their own working tools and entrenching tools for at least 500 infantrymen. Until the reorganisation of 1812, the military workers of the British Army did not have their own wagons for transporting materials and were dependant on the artillery to move their materials. For the Belgian Campaign of 1815, the Royal Sappers and Miners deployed 550 drivers, 160 wagons and 1,000 draught horses. However, only some of the drivers were militarised, coming from the Corps of Royal Artillery Drivers. In addition to the Royal Engineers and the Royal Sappers and Miners, the British Army comprised another technical corps of military engineers: the Royal Staff Corps.

Royal Staff Corps

This was organised in 1798 and was required to provide engineer service under the direct control of the British Army's Commander-in-Chief. In practice, unlike the Royal Engineers and Royal Sappers who were scattered in small detachments across the British Empire, the Royal Staff Corps was to act as the unified engineer force of the British Army's General Staff. Initially, it consisted of four companies, but was later expanded to become a battalion. Its officers had a lot in common with the Royal Engineers and were usually employed singularly. The rankers performed the same functions as the Royal Sappers and Miners.

Each company of the Royal Staff Corps included a sergeant major and a quartermaster sergeant; its rankers were all paid more than the standard infantrymen of the British Army and enjoyed an elite status, for example, when compared with the Royal Sappers. Being a redundant military unit, the Royal Staff Corps was disbanded in 1837 and its members were absorbed into the Royal Engineers and Royal Sappers.

In addition to the Corps of Royal Artillery Drivers, the British Army incorporated a Royal Waggon Train that was tasked with transporting all the materials for the army that did not belong to the artillery. This was organised in 1798, mostly with men drafted from the cavalry, and initially consisted of three troops. Each comprised the following elements: three sergeants, three corporals, one trumpeter, three artificers and 62 privates.

Staff Corps of Cavalry

During the Napoleonic Wars, the Royal Waggon Train was progressively expanded and, by 1814, it was structured on 14 troops with around 1,900 men. Generally, the drivers of the Royal Waggon Train were not known for their discipline and efficiency. Among the technical corps of the British Army that took part in the Napoleonic Wars were the Staff Corps of Cavalry, which was the first military police unit ever formed in Britain.

While operating in the Iberian Peninsula, Wellington realised it was essential to organise a 'provost corps' that could enforce discipline among the British soldiers operating in Spain and Portugal. At that time, it helped to preserve the rights of the local populations from frequent minor crimes committed by the British soldiers. In 1813, four troops of mounted military policemen were organised and became known as the Staff Corps of Cavalry. Two were with Wellington's army in Spain, one was raised in England and one in Ireland. The members of the two troops deployed in the Iberian Peninsula were all volunteers from the cavalry regiments, and had an exemplary reputation. In total, these comprised the following elements: four captains, four lieutenants, two cornets, six sergeants, six corporals and 120 troopers.

The new military policemen had to prevent desertion and looting, but were also tasked with other auxiliary duties. They received an extra pay for their services and wore a distinctive uniform. In 1814, the Staff Corps of Cavalry was disbanded when the British Army left the Iberian Peninsula. It was temporarily re-formed during the following year with two troops and took part in the Belgian Campaign (before being disbanded again in 1818).

Left: Officer of the Royal Engineers wearing the jacket with the frontal lapels buttoned up.

Right: Officer (left) and private (right) of the Royal Waggon Train. (ASKB)

Below left: Officer of the Royal Engineers wearing the jacket with the frontal lapels unbuttoned. (ASKB)

Below right: Trooper of the Staff Corps of Cavalry.

Marines

Until 1755, the naval infantry component of the Royal Navy was provided by several infantry regiments that were detached from the rest of the British Army for sea service. This practice of using standard infantry units to perform naval infantry duties began in 1664, when the famous Duke of York and Albany's Maritime Regiment of Foot was raised. This unit, also known as the Admiral Regiment, provided the needed infantrymen for several warships in the English Navy. In 1755, the British government organised an independent corps of naval infantry, which received the official denomination of Marines (Royal Marines in 1802). The new naval infantrymen were initially structured on 15 autonomous companies, each of which could be sent to serve on one warship. Unlike the sailors of the Royal Navy, the Marines were all volunteers, like the infantrymen of the army and had much in common with them (including the uniform). The various companies of Marines were assembled, at least from an administrative point of view, into three divisions that each took its name from the location where it was based: Chatham, Portsmouth and Plymouth. In 1805, a fourth division was organised at Woolwich.

By that date, the general organisation of the Royal Marines was as follows: 47 companies in the Chatham Division, 48 companies in the Portsmouth Division, 48 companies in the Plymouth Division and 30 companies in the Woolwich Division.

Each company comprised: one captain, two first-lieutenants, two second-lieutenants, eight sergeants, eight corporals, five drummers and 130 privates (increased to 140 in 1808). By December 1815, the total number of companies had been gradually reduced to 80. Until 1804, each of the three divisions that existed at that time comprised: one company of grenadiers and one company of light infantry, but these were later transformed into ordinary companies.

The Royal Marines played a key military role during the Napoleonic Wars and on several occasions supported the British Army by fighting as standard line infantry. Their main tasks, however, were: acting as marksmen on the warships, conducting boarding operations, manning the guns of the warships on which they served and organising amphibious landings. In addition, they had to prevent or crush mutinies among the sailors of a warship.

During 1810, a 1st Battalion of Marines was formed by assembling six companies. A 2nd Battalion was created in July 1812, also with six companies, and a 3rd Battalion (having ten companies) was added in January 1814. These were specifically created to operate in North America, in the War of 1812. The first two battalions arrived in North America during June 1813, while the last was sent in June 1814. In May 1814, shortly before the arrival of the 3rd Battalion, the 2nd Battalion was broken up and its men assigned to other functions. As a result, the 3rd Battalion became the new 2nd Battalion and a new 3rd Battalion was formed by assembling two existing corps of Colonial Marines. The First Corps of Colonial Marines was formed in 1808, while the Second Corps of Colonial Marines was raised in 1814. Both units were made up of freed slaves who came from British possessions in the West Indies. Since most of the regular Royal Marines were involved in the military operations fought in Europe, the British authorities raised freed slaves for service on the warships operating in the Caribbean. The new 3rd Battalion of Royal Marines formed from the Colonial Marines was disbanded in 1815, when the hostilities with the US came to an end.

Until 1804, the guns of the Royal Navy's warships were manned by the Marines or by the sailors embarked on each vessel. This sometimes caused difficulties since a specific level of competence was needed to fire the naval guns of a warship in an effective way. As a result, in August of that year, a new corps known as Royal Marine Artillery was formed. This corps was part of the Royal Marines, but its members were naval artillerymen and not naval infantrymen. Each of the four divisions of Royal Marines had one company of Royal Marine Artillery. A single company comprised: one captain, three first-lieutenants, five second-lieutenants, eight sergeants, five corporals, eight bombardiers, three drummers and 62 gunners.

Above left: **Officer of the Royal Marines. (ASKB)**

Above right: **Private of the Royal Marines. (ASKB)**

Chapter 9

Foreign Troops

At the outbreak of the Revolutionary Wars, the British Army comprised one single unit made up of foreign professional soldiers – the 60th Regiment of Foot (see one of the previous chapters). With the expansion of the military operations conducted against France, however, the Crown was obliged to raise a large number of mercenary corps from foreign sources in order to augment the numerical consistency of the regular forces and to provide the troops that were absent in the British Army (most notably light infantry). During 1793–1802, these were mostly made up of French Royalists, who were forced to abandon their country after the execution of Louis XVI and who were collectively known as émigrés. During the last months of 1794, the French Republic invaded the Netherlands and transformed it into a puppet Batavian Republic; As a result of this event, a large number of Dutch soldiers became available for British service as foreign mercenaries. Several units of 'strangers' were also raised from Germany and Switzerland, two countries that had always exported mercenaries and could contribute expert light infantrymen to the British cause. In 1802, following the Peace of Amiens, most of the foreign corps belonging to the first generation were disbanded. During the following years, however, several new foreign units were raised by the British Army on the new fronts.

Following is a brief overview of the major foreign units that served under the British flag during 1803–15.

King's Dutch Brigade

In 1795, following the fall of the Dutch Republic, the 'stadtholter' William V (1748–1806) fled to Great Britain together with his son Frederick of Orange-Nassau (1774–1799). Frederick was a capable military commander and soon started planning the organisation of a Dutch Army in exile. The army was raised from the Dutch troops who had abandoned their home country and entered Prussian territory to evade capture. In 1795, Prussia was a neutral country. Frederick's loyal soldiers moved to (British) Hanover and were later transferred to Britain, where some were absorbed into foreign units serving in the British Army. During the 1799 Netherlands Campaign, which ended in failure, the British captured several soldiers of the Batavian Republic. These included deserters and mutineers who were united with the Dutch soldiers already in Britain to form a large and independent Dutch military corps.

Uniforms of the King's Dutch Brigade: fusilier of the line infantry (left), light infantryman of the line infantry (centre) and jager (right).

The King's Dutch Brigade was organised with the following units: four regiments of line infantry with 18 companies each, one regiment of jagers (hunters) with 18 companies, one battalion of artillery with six companies and a small engineer corps with one company of pioneers. The Dutch Brigade, comprising 5,000 soldiers, was commanded by Frederick of

Orange-Nassau. In November 1800, the engineers/pioneers were absorbed into the artillery and a second artillery battalion with four companies was created. In addition, the two light companies of each line infantry regiment were detached to create two new jager battalions with four companies each. In 1802, due to the Peace of Amiens, the Dutch Brigade was disbanded without having seen action.

Dutch Light Infantry Battalion
This was organised in January 1814, from Dutch prisoners-of-war stationed in Britain. It consisted of a single battalion with 1,000 men and soon became part of the re-formed Dutch Army as the 2nd Line Infantry Battalion.

Dillon's Regiment
Raised in 1795, this initially consisted of two battalions with five companies each and was mostly made up of Irish soldiers who had served in France's Royal Army. During the Napoleonic Wars, it comprised men from 22 different nationalities. In 1812, it had an establishment of 1,200 soldiers and five of its companies were sent to serve in the Iberian Peninsula. The regiment was disbanded during January 1815.

Froberg's Regiment
Recruited in the Balkans during 1806, it initially had 500 men and was sent to Malta to be part of the local garrison. In April 1807, the unit mutinied and was disbanded a few weeks later.

Foreign Recruits Battalion
This corps was raised in Spain during 1810, from deserters and prisoners of various nationalities. It was used to create the 8th Battalion of the 60th Foot Regiment.

Chasseurs Britanniques
This light infantry unit was created in 1801, by absorbing the remnants of several émigré corps that had just been disbanded. Initially it consisted of six companies. In 1803, it absorbed all the French Royalist soldiers who continued to serve under the British flag and could be expanded to a standard establishment of ten companies. Sent to the Iberian Peninsula, it served with distinction under Wellington during some important battles. The unit was disbanded in 1814. The French Royalists also formed two Foreign Invalids Companies during 1801–14.

Malta Coast Artillery
This little corps consisted of two companies that were charged with manning the coastal batteries of Malta. It was formed from local militiamen in 1800, after the British reoccupied the island.

Maltese Provincial Battalions
These were raised for garrison duty on their home island in 1802 and consisted of seven infantry companies across two batallions. They were commanded by Maltese officers and were unified into a single corps in 1806, then disbanded in 1815.

Maltese Veteran Battalion
Created in 1803, this battalion consisted of 300 Maltese soldiers who were no longer fit for active service. Its four garrison companies were disbanded in 1815.

Maltese Military Artificers
This small auxiliary corps was made up of Maltese soldiers. It consisted of two companies, raised in 1806.

Maltese Police Corps
This was a small para-military corps, comprising around 200 men who acted as a gendarmerie for the island of Malta.

Royal Regiment of Malta
Initially raised as a two-battalion corps in 1805, it was later reduced to a single battalion with 750 men. In 1811, the unit was disbanded, after suffering serious losses in various Mediterranean operations.

Royal Corsican Rangers
This light infantry corps was mostly formed by Corsican soldiers, who fought for the independence of their island from France. Raised in 1803, it consisted of ten companies and most of its officers were Corsican. The corps took part with distinction in several military operations conducted in Southern Italy, before being augmented to 12 companies in 1811. After participating in the British landings at Trieste (1813) and Genoa (1814), the Royal Corsican Rangers was disbanded in 1816.

Royal Sicilian Regiment
After the French invaded the Kingdom of Naples in southern Italy during 1806, the local Bourbon royal family withdrew to the island of Sicily where it continued to resist the invaders. At that time, Sicily was the richest region of the Bourbon's southern Italian kingdom and had large human resources. It could easily be defended from the French by the Royal Navy. In May 1806, the British authorities in Sicily started raising a light infantry battalion from Sicilian volunteers; this was gradually expanded to ten and later 12 companies, becoming a regiment in 1809, and serving as part of Sicily's garrison until being disbanded in 1816.

Calabrian Free Corps
From 1806, the main theatre of operations between the French and the Bourbons of Naples (supported by Britain) was the southern tip of Calabria, which was located in front of the eastern Sicilian coast. The French and their puppet Kingdom of Naples, ruled by Joachim Murat (1767–1815), wanted to invade Sicily. Thanks to the British naval presence in the area, however, this was never achieved. The Calabrian Free Corps was organised, in 1809, from Bourbon subjects of Calabria who were still loyal to their royal family. Initially, it consisted of just four companies, but since the Calabrian mountaineers were probably the best light infantrymen in the Mediterranean, it was rapidly expanded to 15 companies. Six of these served with distinction under Wellington in Spain, six were sent to the Ionian Islands as garrison troops, and three remained in Sicily. In 1814, after taking part in the British occupation of Genoa, the Calabrian Free Corps was disbanded.

Italian Levy
Around 1810, there were thousands of Italian prisoners-of-war in Britain, who were against Napoleon and who had been enlisted in his Italian troops by force. In 1811, these were assembled and sent to Malta, where they were organised by Lieutenant-General Lord William Bentick (1774–1839) into a new corps known as Italian Levy. This initially consisted of a single infantry regiment with two battalions of four companies each. In May 1812, this 1st Italian Regiment was supplemented by a 2nd Italian Regiment, which included many soldiers from a disbanded infantry regiment of the Sicilian Army (the Reggimento

Real Estero). A 3rd Italian Regiment was organised during 1813 and the raising of a fourth was planned but never realised. All three units of the Italian Levy had full establishments by early 1814.

The 1st Italian Regiment served in Spain and fought with distinction during the British landings at Trieste (1813) and at Genoa (1814). The 2nd Italian Regiment also served in Spain, but was disarmed for bad conduct. In 1815, the entire Italian Levy fought in Piedmont against the French who wanted to invade the re-established Kingdom of Sardinia. Following the end of hostilities, it was proposed the three regiments be absorbed into the Piedmontese Army, but these plans came to nothing and the Italian Levy was disbanded during 1816.

Piedmontese Legion

The Savoy royal house of Piedmont had been obliged to abandon its kingdom after it was occupied by the French troops of Napoleon. As a result, it withdrew to the island of Sardinia, which was part of the Piedmontese state from the early 18th century. Here, the Savoy king could reorganise his military forces and continue his resistance against the French, with the decisive support of the Royal Navy that protected Sardinia from French landings. In 1813, in view of the imminent liberation of Piedmont from French rule, the British organised a new military unit made up of Italian prisoners-of-war (like the Italian Levy) that would have served under the Savoy flag. Known as Piedmontese Legion, it consisted of two infantry battalions with six companies each. When the unit reached Genoa, hostilities had already ceased in Europe and it was made part of the newly re-organised Piedmontese Army (later disbanded, in 1817).

Ionian Islands Volunteer Militia

Until 1797, the Ionian Islands, an archipelago with a strategic position in the Adriatic Sea, had been part of the Venetian Republic. When the republic was occupied by Napoleon's troops, the Ionian Islands were annexed to France. In 1799, a joint Russian-Ottoman fleet occupied the archipelago and the islands were reorganised as the autonomous Septinsular Republic, under a Russian-Ottoman protectorate. In 1807, following the Treaty of Tilsit, the Russians ceded the Ionian Islands to France. In 1810, however, the Royal Navy conquered the archipelago and occupied it until the end of the Napoleonic Wars. During 1815–64, the Ionian Islands were organised as the United States of the Ionian Islands, a British protectorate which suzerainty was ceded to Greece only in 1864. In the years 1810–15, the British organised an irregular local militia in the archipelago, which comprised a total of 4,000 fighters, half of which came from the island of Zante.

1st Regiment of Greek Light Infantry

After capturing the Ionian Islands from the French in March 1810, the British raised an infantry unit made up of local soldiers (Greeks and Albanians). This initially comprised just five companies, later increased to ten. The unit was disbanded in 1816, after taking part in the British occupation of Genoa in 1814. Several future leaders of the Greek War of Independence fought in the ranks of this corps.

2nd Regiment of Greek Light Infantry

Organised in 1813, it originally had just four companies. Like the other Greek regiment, most of its officers were Greek and not British. The unit was disbanded in 1814.

Private of the Greek Light Infantry.

Meuron Regiment

This mercenary Swiss regiment had originally been part of the Dutch Army. Raised in 1781, it briefly campaigned with the French in South Africa during 1783 and was later stationed in Ceylon from 1786. In 1795, the regiment was captured by the British and entered into its service. Its standard establishment was of ten companies. In 1813, the unit was sent to Canada and fought in the war of 1812 against the USA. The Meuron Regiment was disbanded in 1816 and many of its members settled in Canada as colonists.

Roll Regiment

This mercenary Swiss regiment was raised in December 1794 for British service. Initially, it had two battalions, which were reduced to one during 1798. In 1809, it absorbed 400 Swiss soldiers who had been captured in Spain and had previously served in the Napoleonic military forces. With these new recruits, the regiment was expanded to 12 companies (one of which was equipped with rifles). Part of the unit served with distinction in Spain, before the whole regiment was disbanded in 1816.

Watteville Regiment

This Swiss mercenary regiment was raised in 1801 and from its beginning it had ten companies. The inclusion of several prisoners of war enabled the formation of two additional companies in 1810. During 1813, the Watteville Regiment was transferred to Canada for service in the War of 1812 against the USA. The unit took part in several of the most important battles fought during the that conflict. It was disbanded in 1816, but some of its members settled in Canada as colonists.

The following were the foreign cavalry/artillery units that served under the British flag during the period 1800–15:

York Hussars

Raised in 1793, this unit was mostly made up of German soldiers and consisted of three squadrons with two companies each (for a total of 600 men). After taking part in the Flanders Campaign, it was sent to Haiti, where it suffered heavy casualties. Before returning to Britain in 1799, it absorbed several foreigners who had been part of recently disbanded cavalry corps. The York Hussars was disbanded in July 1802.

Hompesch's Mounted Rifles

Raised by Charles de Hompesch during 1796, in Germany, this unit consisted of four troops with 114 men each. It took part in the military operations of the 1798 Irish Rebellion and in the Egyptian Campaign. The corps was disbanded in September 1802.

Minorca Light Dragoons

A short-lived light cavalry company raised from some Hungarians during the British occupation of Minorca. It was disbanded in 1802 after less than two years of service.

Foreign Hussars

Formed during 1810, in Sicily, by assembling all the soldiers of the foreign units in British service serving on the island who could ride a horse. It consisted of a single troop that was attached to the 20th Light Dragoons and was deployed in the Iberian Peninsula until being disbanded in 1813.

King's German Legion

Among all the non-native troops at the service of Great Britain during the Napoleonic Wars, the King's German Legion (KGL) was the largest and best of all. It was a sort of miniature army comprising military units of every kind and fought with great valour during most of Wellington's campaign. The German soldiers of the KGL were considered as the best professionals of the British Army, together with the members of a few elite corps such as the Foot Guards. As noted, the German state of Hanover was in personal union with the Kingdom of Great Britain since the early 18th century, and thus the two countries were ruled by the same monarch. In practice, however, they had different institutions and were governed as two autonomous states. Hanover had its own army and its own administration. It is clear, however, that during the European conflicts of the 18th century Hanover always fought on Britain's side. Bordering with France, it was always exposed to foreign invasions and had to count on British military support on several occasions to preserve its territorial integrity. Among the military forces of the German states, the Hanoverian Army was one of the most efficient and professional. At the outbreak of the Revolutionary Wars, it comprised the following units:

- one regiment of Guard infantry, mustering two battalions with six companies each (one of grenadiers, five of musketeers) plus an artillery section with four guns
- 15 regiments of line infantry, mustering two battalions with six companies each (one of grenadiers, five of musketeers) plus an artillery section with four guns
- one regiment of Guard cavalry, across four squadrons with two companies each
- four regiments of heavy cavalry, across four squadrons with two companies each
- 4 regiments of dragoons, across four squadrons with two companies each
- two regiments of light dragoons, across four squadrons with two companies each
- one regiment of artillery, across two battalions with five companies each
- one Miner and Sapper Company
- one Pontoon and Pioneer Company

The Hanoverian Army, the German one, lacked light infantry troops in 1793 just like the British one. As war with France progressed, however, one of the line infantry regiments was converted into a light infantry corps. This was structured with two battalions each with six companies, two of jagers and four of standard light infantrymen. In addition, several grenadier companies from the existing infantry regiments were detached from their original units and assembled to form three elite battalions of grenadiers (each of these having four companies). In 1803, after hostilities resumed between Britain and France, Hanover was invaded by Napoleon's military forces over the course of a few days. Isolated and surrounded by hostile territories, it was practically impossible to defend. The Hanoverian Army was formally disbanded, but thousands of its members were willing to continue the fight against France under the flags of their royal family. As a result, in August 1803, the British government issued a proclamation that invited all the former members of the Hanoverian Army to join the ranks of the British military forces.

The German volunteers assembled into a new corps known as The King's Germans, which preserved the traditions of the recently disbanded Hanoverian Army. During the following weeks, hundreds of volunteers responded to the call and started to leave Germany. Most embarked from the port of Husum on the North Sea and travelled to England over a few days. So many volunteers came from Germany that it soon became clear that a new fighting force comprising all arms could be formed. The depot of the new corps was initially placed on the Isle of Wight, but was transferred to Portsmouth because of the increasingly large number of recruits. By December 1803, the new unit of the British Army had received its official denomination of KGL.

During 1804, the KGL continued to be expand with the arrival of new volunteers and was gradually organised as a perfectly trained military force. By mid-1805, it had a stable structure that comprised the following units:

- four battalions of line infantry
- two battalions of light infantry
- one regiment of dragoons
- two regiments of light dragoons
- three companies (batteries) of foot artillery
- two companies (batteries) of horse artillery
- Engineer Corps (made up of a few specialised officers)

The internal organisation of these units was exactly the same as their British counterparts. Officers were mostly German and the discipline of the rankers was excellent. The two battalions of light infantry had one third of their members armed with rifled carbines, while the rest were equipped with light infantry smoothbore muskets. Each of the line infantry battalions included an elite platoon of sharpshooters (50 men), who were armed with rifles. In 1805, while Napoleon was fighting against the Austrians and the Russians in Central Europe, Britain assembled an expeditionary force with the objective of reconquering Hanover. This comprised 6,000 soldiers from the KGL and it was able to occupy Hanover without much fighting. At that time the French were heavily involved on other fronts. When Napoleon triumphed at Austerlitz, however, this situation changed and the British expeditionary force had to leave Germany to avoid a direct confrontation with the French Army.

The few months spent in Hanover had very positive consequence for the KGL: thousands of local volunteers joined the unit and followed it during the retreat to Britain. Thanks to the new recruits, it was possible to organise the following additional units:

- four battalions of line infantry
- one regiment of dragoons
- one regiment of light dragoons
- one company (battery) of foot artillery

In 1807, the KGL was sent to Denmark as part of the British military force that attacked Copenhagen. In 1808, it was transported to the Iberian Peninsula where it remained until 1814. In Spain, the German soldiers of Britain took part in all the most decisive battles fought against the French and on several occasions, it was their great courage and outstanding discipline that determined the outcome of a clash. Wellington, who commanded these men for years, considered them to be the best of his troops. The soldiers of the KGL were able to endure hardship, and despite suffering losses of every kind they always retained very high morale. In 1815, after having participated in the occupation of southern France, the KGL fought its last campaign in Belgium. The corps had already been transferred to Flanders when the hostilities with France resumed and its destiny had not yet been decided: Hanover had been freed by the French and was now rebuilding its national army; it would have been obvious to use the KGL as the main core of the Hanoverian Army, but Wellington wanted to keep the veterans of the KGL as part of the British Army. During the few months of Napoleon's first exile, the internal strength of the KGL units was greatly reduced but no corps were disbanded. The companies in each infantry battalion were reduced from ten to six, while the troops in each cavalry regiment were reduced from eight to six. The 7,000 remaining soldiers of the corps were involved into the Battle of Waterloo and fought with great distinction. In particular, they defended the key position of La Haye Sainte (a farm) to the last man, enabling Wellington to win the battle.

In December 1815, with the Napoleonic Wars over, the KGL was ordered to march home to Hanover. Here all the units of the corps were disbanded during the first months of 1816. Most of the officers and men who had served under Wellington enlisted in the new Hanoverian Army that was in the process of being re-organised. The many battle honours of the KGL were inherited by the new Hanoverian units, which acquired a great amount of competence and experience thanks to the inclusion of these veterans.

The Hanoverian Army of 1815 was structured as follows:

- nine battalions of line infantry
- 30 battalions of militia infantry
- three regiments of hussars
- three companies (batteries) of foot artillery

The nine regular infantry battalions were grouped together with three battalions of militia infantry to form larger infantry corps then divided into three brigades with four companies each.

Chapter 10
Uniforms

Above left: Detail of a line infantry officer's sword. (Photo and © His Majesty's 33rd Regiment of Foot)

Above middle: Example of M1812 shako. (Photo and © 32nd Cornwall Regiment of Foot)

Above right: Example of M1812 shako. (Photo and © 44th East Essex Regiment of Foot)

Infantry uniform

The British Army infantry of 1800–15 wore the smartest and most distinctive uniforms of their age. These were practical and modern for the time, especially when compared to those used by other armies that were still produced according to the military fashions of the 18th century. Red, the characteristic colour of the British infantry since the years of Cromwell's New Model Army, was retained for most of the regiments, but several of the new light infantry corps received innovative uniforms in dark green colour. Also, several foreign corps did not wear the standard red dress of the national line infantry, thus presenting a quite distinctive appearance. A basic description for each item of dress used by the British foot troops is provided.

Headgear

Bicorn

The standard headgear for the officers was the cocked hat. Its original shape had three folds but now the standard issue was bicorn with two folds. This change occurred during the last decades of the 18th century, so that by 1800 all British officers worn the bicorn. The left turn-up held a black cockade (decorative ribbon), held in place by a loop and a button of the same colour. During the previous decades, the cocked hats had always featured metallic lace around the external edges, but by 1800 this had disappeared. Above the black cockade was a plume, its colours indicating the company in which an officer was serving. Red in the bottom part and white in the top indicated a centre company; an entirely white plume indicated a grenadier company; and an entirely green plume indicated a light infantry company. The bicorn was worn with the loop over the left eye and with the right wing thrown a little forward. Sometimes the loop could be in the distinctive colour of the regiment, but this practice became popular only during the second half of the Napoleonic Wars. Each cocked hat had two cords that passed around its crown to tighten it or to pull in the sides, but over time these became purely decorative. The cords were golden and at their ends was a tassel of the same colour. Each cord passed through the loop of the other, with the golden tassel hanging from a lock in the hat. To prevent the bicorn from falling off, two narrow tapes were sewn into its lining and passed down (around the back of the head) to be joined by a hook and eye.

Shako (1800)

In 1811, the cocked hat was replaced as the standard headgear of the officers by the shako, which had been issued to NCOs and soldiers since February 1800. Until that date, the rankers had worn the bicorn albeit with some minor differences to that described above (for example, in the colour of the cords). Before the introduction of the shako, the British infantrymen had already tested alternative headgear that could have replaced the old bicorn.

The shako was a black round hat made of felt, with a broad curved brim edged with tape and supported by rigid strips coming from the crown. It had a black band wrapped around the base and a cockade of the same colour placed on the right side of the crown. Over the cockade was a plume in company colours. During the Revolutionary Wars against France, the round hat became very popular, since it was practical and easier to wear than the bicorn. However, it was never adopted by the whole infantry. Sometimes it could be adorned by a bearskin crest, running from front to back like the helmets of the light cavalry.

The M1800 shako was commonly known as 'stovepipe' shako because of its distinctive shape; its introduction was innovative for the time, and the British Army was one of the first in the world to adopt the shako as standard headgear. The French Army of Napoleon, for example, introduced it on a large scale in 1806. It was made of lacquered leather and had a flat peak on the front; the crown had a cylindrical shape, which resembled that of a stovepipe. Very frequently, the M1800 shako had a black neck protector on the back, made of leather or oilcloth. This could be tucked up into the hat or hooked up when not in use. On the top of the crown were cut feathers for officers or a worsted wool tuft for other ranks, in company colour. At the base of the feathers/tuft was a black horsehair or leather cockade, which carried a small button with regimental number at its centre. Instead of the number, the button of grenadier companies bore a flaming grenade, while that of light companies bore a bugle horn. The front of the shako carried a large plate made of tin, with a specific design die-stamped on the rear. The frontal plate of officers' shakos was secured by copper-gilt shanks, while those of the rankers' shakos had small holes at the edges in order to take thin brass wires that secured the plate to the shako.

The decorations reproduced on the frontal plate included several elements. In the top part there was a crown, with the regimental number to its side. In the central part, was the royal cypher, surrounded by several decorative elements such as laurel branches. At the bottom was a lion, on which the regimental number could be placed.

The infantry regiments bearing the title of royal in their official denomination, the Foot Guards and some other units having a very long regimental history had the privilege of wearing a different frontal plate. This had a distinctive regimental symbol, which varied for each unit.

From 1806, a new version of the shako was produced, which was lighter and slightly shorter but maintained the main features of the previous version. The officers' version of the shako had black lace around the base and a frontal plate made of gilt. Until 1808, the cut feathers on the officer's shako had been taller than the tuft worn on the ranker's, but in that year their dimensions matched the shorter version.

Shako (1812)

In March 1812, a new model of shako was introduced, which was more comfortable as well as practical to wear on the battlefield. It became known as Belgian shako or Waterloo shako, since it was used on a large scale by most of the British infantry during the Belgian campaign of 1815. The main feature of this new headgear was that it had a crown that sloped at the back, producing a false front. On the rear, the crown was also broader. Like the previous shako, it was made of black felt for the rankers. For the NCOs, it was produced with coarse beaver, while for the officers it was made of fine beaver. The false front was edged with black lace and on the front of the headgear there was a peak made of lacquered leather. An additional band of black lace was frequently worn around the bottom part of the headgear, especially by officers.

Neck protectors remained in use and could be suspended from a cord at the rear. The M1812 shako had a feather tuft for officers and a worsted tuft for other ranks, always in company colour. The tuft was now worn on the left side of the shako (something that made it much more practical). At its base was the black cockade, held in place by a button. It bore the regimental number for centre companies, a flaming grenade for grenadier companies and a bugle horn for light infantry companies. A black oilskin cover was usually worn over the shako for protection, especially during winters spent on campaign. A small and separate cover of the same material could be worn over the tuft. Unlike the previous model, this shako had no chinstrap, but one could be added. On the front of the shako, was a twist cord with a tassel at each end; a doubled loop knot was formed to shorten the cord into two lengths of chain with an un-knotted length at the centre. The cord was worn with the doubled loop end hooked behind the cockade, with a length of loop knots at each side of the shako plate and the two tassels on the right. This cord was golden for officers, white for centre and grenadier companies, and green for light companies. Very frequently, the decorative cord was not worn on campaign. The frontal plate of the M1812 shako was made of copper-gilt for officers and of brass for other ranks. The standard badge reproduced on the plate comprised a crown in the top part, a royal cypher in the central part (of a simpler design than that of the M1800 shako) and the regimental number in the bottom part. Sometimes it featured a lion between the royal cypher and the regimental number. The Foot Guards, the royal regiments and some other units wore their distinctive symbols on the frontal plate as it had been for the previous model of headgear. In December 1814, the light infantry regiments and the light companies of the line regiments replaced the frontal plates of their shakos with two separate badges: one reproduced a bugle horn and the other reproduced the unit number. Both were silver.

Fur caps

The grenadiers, sappers and musicians of the line infantry units could wear a tall fur cap that made them very easy to recognise on the field of battle; however, it was usually used only during parades or on other special occasions since it was impractical to wear. The fur cap, used until 1802, had the fur rising towards the top in a tapered point and on the rear it carried a red patch that was often embroidered with the regimental number or symbol (usually in white). On the front the fur cap had a black lacquered plate, with red lace on the bottom edge and some white metal decorations. They usually consisted of the United Kingdom's coat of arms, with the letters 'GR' for the monarch on the sides and under the words 'Nec Aspera Terrent' (They are not afraid of difficulties). The pattern of the decorations, however, could vary from unit to unit. Sometimes, the lacquered plate could be red (2nd Foot Guards) or white (3rd Foot Guards). The fur cap was also decorated with knotted worsted cords and tassels, which ran on the front and on the back in an oblique way. The cords and tassels were silver for officers, gilt for NCOs and white for rankers. On the back of the cap, under the red patch, was a metal badge – a flaming grenade for grenadiers, a crossed axe and saw for sappers, and a drum for musicians. On the left side, the fur cap had a small white plume.

In 1802, the fur cap was replaced by a new model, which was much taller and heavily influenced by the bearskin caps used by the contemporary French grenadiers. This new headgear was rounded at the top and had the fur running downwards. On the back of it there was no coloured patch, while the decorative cords and tassels were retained as well as the metal badge worn on the back. The white plume, placed on the left side of the headgear, was much taller than that of the pre-1802 model. During the last years of the Napoleonic Wars, chin scales were added to the fur cap, which were often worn fastened up at the front or back. The frontal plate of the M1802 fur cap was the same for all regiments and bore the royal arms; it was copper gilt for officers and NCOs, while for rankers it was brass. Like the previous fur cap, it was worn on parade or for special occasions.

Kilmarnock bonnet

The standard headgear of the Highland regiments was the Kilmarnock bonnet, which was dark blue and could be fitted with a removable peak on the front if required. Around the Kilmarnock there was a chequered band of white, red and green or a chequered band of white and red known as Southerland dicing. On the back of the bonnet were two black tails, placed on the neck. On the top was a pompom (known as toorie) and made of wool. This was white for grenadiers, red for fusiliers and green for light companies. In addition, the Kilmarnock could be or have some decorative black ostrich feathers. These were sewn around the stiff blue cloth of the cap, and were of two different kinds – shorter flats and longer foxtails. The foxtails curved over the flats to provide the required fullness. The feathers (clipped and fastened on a stem) were worn on the left of the Kilmarnock and were held in position by a black cockade, which had a metal button that bore the regimental number for centre companies, a flaming grenade for grenadiers, and a bugle horn for light companies.

Over time, features of the Kilmarnock were changed. The number of black ostrich feathers increased (they were also more curved towards the top of the headgear), and a plume was added on the left of the bonnet. This was held in place by the black cockade and was white for grenadier companies, white over red for centre companies and green for light companies. The plumes of flank companies were longer than those of battalion companies. The 42nd Regiment of Foot was the only one to have different colours for the plumes: entirely red for fusiliers, red over white for grenadiers and red over green for light companies. On campaign, a flat version of the Kilmarnock bonnet was frequently worn; this was dark blue and bore the black cockade near the toorie, but had no tails on the back and no chequered band. Apparently, the grenadiers of the Highland regiments wore their parade fur caps much more frequently than the grenadiers of the English or Lowland regiments.

Peculiar uniforms

5th Battalion of the 60th Foot Regiment

From their origins, the light infantry corps of the British Army had distinctive uniforms and did not wear the same headgear as the line infantry. The 5th Battalion of the 60th Foot Regiment was the first to have distinctive dress, and its headgear consisted of a black Tarleton helmet for officers and a black stovepipe shako for other ranks. The helmet had a black peak on the front and a fur crest that went across its crown from front to back. It was decorated by a band of dark green cloth with silver stripes that was wrapped around its bottom part and by a plume of the same colour that was placed on the left side and held in position by a red cockade. The shako was black, with a small dark green plume on the front held in place by a red cockade. On the front of the headgear was also a silver bugle horn badge. Decorative dark green cords and tassels were frequently worn around the shako, while the helmet could have a silver bugle horn badge applied on the right side.

95th Rifles

After being raised, the 95th Rifles adopted the same kinds of headgear described above, albeit with some small differences. The cockade, for example, was black for both the officer's helmet and for the stovepipe shako.

Above left: Detail of the lace embroidered on the buttonholes of the line infantry's jacket. (Photo and © His Majesty's 33rd Regiment of Foot)

Above middle: Detail of the lace embroidered on the round cuffs of the line infantry's jacket. (Photo © His Majesty's 33rd Regiment of Foot)

Above right: Detail of a Brown Bess musket. (Photo and © His Majesty's 33rd Regiment of Foot)

Below: Brown Bess musket of the so-called Short Land Pattern (used by light infantry regiments/companies). (Photo and © 2nd Battalion, 95th Rifles)

Rifles and light infantry regiments

Later, the 60th Regiment adopted new black cockades. When the new M1812 shako was introduced for the line infantry, the 60th Foot and the 95th Rifles maintained their stovepipe shakos as a mark of distinction from all the other foot units. The original headgear for rankers was never modified in a significant way; the only notable innovation was in the unit badge worn on the front. This was made of brass and, in addition to the bugle horn, it bore the unit number. For the officers, the Tarleton helmet was in use for a very short time since it was impractical to wear on campaign. It was replaced by the stovepipe shako employed by rankers. The light infantry regiments that were created by converting existing line units retained their standard stovepipe shakos; these continued to be worn after the introduction of the new M1812 headgear, as a mark of distinction. They followed the same evolution as the shakos used by the rifle corps and had the same frontal badge with bugle horn. However, for the light regiments formed of former Highland line units, a peculiar version of the stovepipe shako was made, which had several features of the Scottish Kilmarnock. It was dark blue and had a chequered band of white, red and green; it had the same frontal badge of the ordinary shakos but instead of the frontal plume it had a dark green toorie on the top.

Coats/jackets

In 1793, the British infantry wore long-tailed coats, which were worn open from the neck and sloped away at the waist. The main colour of this item of dress was scarlet, with collar, cuffs and lapels in the distinctive colour of each regiment. The facings were white except for those regiments that had buff as their distinctive colour (and they had buff facings). The skirt and linings over which the coat was worn were white for most of the regiments and buff for those with buff facings. The scarlet coats had horizontal pockets for centre and grenadier companies, while those of the light companies were oblique. Each coat could be worn with the lapels buttoned over or folded back in order to show the regiment's colour; the former practice was popular only on campaign and mostly among the light companies of the various regiments.

In 1796, this model of coat, which had not changed since the days of the American Revolution, was overhauled to be much more practical and modern. Now it was to be fastened to the waist; the lapels were retained (for the moment) but were made to button over on every occasion. The collar was modified to be a standing one, instead of lying flat. In October 1797, the lapels were officially removed for all non-officers and thus the scarlet coat of the British line infantry became a single-breasted jacket. The British Army had been one of the most innovative in Europe and one of the first in the world to replace the old coats with a new item of dress. The latter no longer had tails (which were replaced by 'false' tails) but continued to have horizontal pockets for centre and grenadier companies or oblique ones for light companies.

On the front, the new jacket had five pairs of buttons; four on each cuff and pocket. All the 26 buttons of the jacket had white lace, while the collar was piped in white. All the modifications described, introduced from 1796–97, became official with the dress regulations of 1802. The general appearance of the new uniform was extremely smart. The standing collar and round cuffs were in the distinctive colour of each regiment, as well as the shoulder straps, which were piped in white. The piping had been present on the pre-1796 uniform, but now included a white crest sewn to the shoulder and pointed at the other end where they were secured, close to the collar, by a small button.

Flank companies did not have shoulder straps but shoulder wings, which were edged in white and padded with wool of the same colour. The jackets of the Highland regiments were slightly different from those of the other units: they had four pairs of buttons on the front and three on each pocket. In addition, all companies of the Highland regiments had oblique pockets.

The jackets worn by officers were different from those used by their men in that they retained their lapels. On most occasions, and especially during campaigns, these were buttoned over, so that the jacket looked like it was double-breasted. On parade, however, it was still possible to fold them back in order to show the distinctive colour of the regiment in a single frontal plastron. The five pairs of buttons placed on the lapels, the single button worn on each side of the collar and the four buttons worn on each cuff or pocket all had golden lace. The false turnbacks of the M1802 jacket were piped in gold for officers and in white for other ranks. In 1793, the musicians of each regiment wore the same uniform as the other soldiers, but with reversed colours. The coat was in the distinctive colour of each regiment, while the facings were scarlet. The musicians of regiments having black as its distinctive colour were the only exception to this rule, since they wore white coats with black facings. Those musicians with white or buff coats were to have scarlet linings instead of the usual white ones. With the introduction of the 1802 dress regulations, all the musicians' jackets were laced on the seams. The colour and decorative design of this distinctive lace was chosen by the commander of each regiment and it was different for each unit. Over time, the musicians' jackets were decorated with stripes of cloth (usually having a 'V' shape) that were worn on the sleeves and had the same colour/decorative design as the lace on the seams. The musicians of the infantry regiments were easy to recognise on the battlefield because they wore the same shoulder wings as the flank companies.

In 1812, another change was made to the uniforms of the musicians: all jackets were to be scarlet just like those of the rank and file soldiers from each regiment and the old practice of wearing reversed colours was abandoned. The 5th Battalion of the 60th Foot was the first regular light infantry unit of the British Army to wear dark green. This included a very modern and smart single-breasted jacket, with red standing collar and pointed cuffs. The piping on the front and the turnbacks on the jacket were red. Shoulder straps were dark green with red piping and had dark green-and-red rolls. The rifle companies of the other battalions from the same regiment wore a slightly different single-breasted jacket: this had a dark green standing collar and pointed cuffs piped in red, entirely dark green rolls on the shoulders and dark green short turnbacks piped in red. Officers wore a completely different uniform, comprising a dark green 'light dragoon' single-breasted jacket with three rows of buttons on the front, connected between them by black frogging. The bottom edge of the jacket was piped in black. The standing collar and pointed cuffs were red, decorated with silver embroidering. The jacket also had silver shoulder wings, piped in red and decorated with silver fringes.

The uniform adopted by the new 95th Rifles in 1800 remained more or less unchanged during the Napoleonic Period. This comprised a dark green jacket with three rows of buttons on the front, the latter soon becoming a distinctive feature of the Rifle corps' dress. The jacket had standing collar and pointed cuffs in black; shoulder straps were dark green, with black piping and crest made of black wool. By 1815, white piping had been added to collar, cuffs and shoulder straps.

The officer's jacket was quite different and consisted of a dolman similar to that worn by the light dragoons. This was dark green and had three rows of buttons on the front; the buttons, however, were smaller and much more numerous than those worn on the jackets of the other ranks. In addition, they were connected by black decorative frogging. Collar and pointed cuffs were black, the former being decorated by an extra stripe of black lace and the latter by an embroidered Hungarian knot. The line infantry regiments that had converted to become light ones retained their standard scarlet uniforms, simply adding shoulder wings to them. In the light regiments they were worn as a mark of distinction by all companies and not only by the flank ones, as in the line regiments. The officers retained their original uniforms like the rankers under their command, but very frequently these underwent some modifications that were not prescribed by official regulations. First of all, many light infantry officers wore the lapels of their jackets folded back also on campaign: this was made to show the frontal plastron in the distinctive colour of the regiment. In addition, light infantry officers frequently wore a hussar jacket (known as pelisse) on their left shoulder. This was usually red or grey and had the external edges covered with fur. Because of its many buttons and decorative frogging, it was a very popular item of dress. It was not uncommon for light infantry officers to wear a green band of cloth wrapped around the bottom part of their shako or to use light cavalry boots instead of the usual infantry ones.

Each foot regiment of the British Army had a distinctive colour for the facings. All the units bearing the title royal in their official denomination had dark blue as the facing colour.

Dark blue
1st, 2nd and 3rd Foot Guards; 1st (The Royal Scots), 2nd (The Queen's Royal), 4th (King's Own), 7th (Royal Fusiliers), 8th (The King's), 18th (The Royal Irish), 21st (Royal North British Fusiliers), 23rd (Royal Welsh Fusiliers), 42nd (Royal Highland), and 60th (Royal American) Regiment of Foot

Above right: Canteen and backpack of the line infantry. (Photo and © 32nd Cornwall Regiment of Foot)

Above middle: Rear view of a line infantryman's personal equipment. (Photo © His Majesty's 33rd Regiment of Foot)

Above right: Canteen of the line infantry. (Photo and © His Majesty's 33rd Regiment of Foot)

Black
50th (West Kent), 58th (Rutlandshire), 64th (2nd Staffordshire), 70th (Surrey [Glasgow Lowland from 1812]), 89th, and 95th Regiment of Foot (Rifles)

Buff
3rd (The Buffs), 14th (Bedfordshire [Buckinghamshire] from 1809), 22nd (Cheshire), 31st (Huntingdonshire), 48th (Northamptonshire), 52nd (Oxfordshire), 61st South Gloucestershire), 62nd (Wiltshire), 71st (Glasgow Highland), 78th (Ross-Shire Buffs), 81st (Loyal Lincoln Volunteers), 96th, 98th, and 103rd Regiment of Foot

Pale buff
27th (Enniskillen), and 104th Regiment of Foot

Deep buff
40th (2nd Somersetshire), and 90th Regiment of Foot (Pertshire Volunteers)

Yellow
13th (1st Somersetshire), 15th (Yorkshire East Riding), 16th (Buckinghamshire [Bedfordshire from 1809]), 28th (North Gloucestershire), 29th (Worcestershire), 34th (Cumberland), 37th (North Hampshire), 38th (1st Staffordshire), 44th (East Essex), 75th, 77th (East Middlesex), 80th (Staffordshire Volunteers), 85th (Bucks Volunteers), 86th (Shropshire Volunteers [Leinster from 1806]), 88th (Connaught Rangers), 92nd (Gordon Highlanders), 93rd (Sutherland Highlanders), 99th (Prince of Wales' Tipperary), 100th (Prince Regent's County of Dublin), and 102nd Regiment of Foot

Deep yellow
6th (1st Warwickshire), 25th (Sussex [King's own Scottish Borderers from 1805]), and 72nd (Seaforth's Highlanders) Regiment of Foot

Pale yellow
9th, (East Norfolk), 10th (North Lincolnshire), 12th (East Suffolk), 20th (East Devonshire) 26th (Cameronian), 30th (Cambridgeshire), 46th (South Devonshire), 57th (West Middlesex), 67th (South Hampshire), 82nd (Prince of Wales' Volunteers), 83rd (County of Dublin), 84th (York and Lancaster), 91st (Argyllshire Highlanders), and 97th (Queen's Own Germans) Regiment of Foot

Yellowish green
5th (Northumberland), and 36th (Herefordshire) Regiment of Foot

Yellow-green
54th (West Norfolk), and 66th (Berkshire) Regiment of Foot

Blue-green
11th (North Devonshire), 19th (1st Yorkshire North Riding), 24th (2nd Warwickshire), 45th (1st Nottinghamshire), 49th (Hertfordshire), 51st (2nd Yorkshire West Riding), 55th (Westmoreland), 63rd (West Suffolk), 68th (Durham), 69th (South Lincolnshire), 87th (Prince of Wales' Irish), 73rd, 79th "Cameron), and 94th (Scotch Brigade) Regiment of Foot

Above left: **Drum of the 33rd Regiment of Foot. (Photo and © His Majesty's 33rd Regiment of Foot)**

Above right: **Drum and flag of the 32nd Regiment of Foot. (Photo and © 32nd Cornwall Regiment of Foot)**

Light green
39th (East Middlesex [Dorsetshire from 1807]) Regiment of Foot

White
17th (Leicestershire), 32nd (Cornwall), 43rd (Monmouthshire), 47th (Lancashire), 59th (2nd Nottinghamshire), 65th (2nd Yorkshire North Riding), 74th, and 101st (Duke of York's Irish) Regiment of Foot

Red
33rd (1st Yorkshire West Riding), 41st (Royal Invalids), 53rd (Shropshire), and 76th Regiment of Foot

Orange
35th (Dorsetshire [Sussex from 1805]) Regiment of Foot

Purple
56th (West Essex) Regiment of Foot

Rank distinctions

An officer's rank was indicated by epaulettes worn on the shoulders. These could be gold or silver, like the buttons on the uniform. Number of epaulettes (one or two) and position (right shoulder or left shoulder) indicated rank. Officers of flank companies wore their epaulettes over fringed shoulder wings, which were gold or silver to match the epaulettes. They also had distinctive company badges over the epaulettes: a flaming grenade for grenadier companies and a bugle horn for light infantry.

In February 1810, the system was partly modified, with the introduction of two new badges (a star and a crown) that were used to identify officer ranks in a more precise way. These new badges were worn on the epaulettes, which continued to be gold or silver. In addition, the epaulettes of the officers from flank companies were produced in a new model that included the shoulder wings (which were no longer a separate component).

- Officers could easily be recognised by a gorget worn under the neck (which could be gold or silver) and a red silk sash worn around the waist. The gorget bore the regiment's number for most units, except for the Foot Guards and for some old regiments that had the privilege of bearing the royal cypher or a regimental symbol
- The red sash was worn over the left shoulder by officers of the Highland regiments
- From 1802, the rank of NCOs and soldiers was indicated with chevrons. Chevrons pointed downwards and were placed on the sleeves mid-way between the shoulder and the elbow. The colour and number of chevrons indicated different ranks; colour sergeants (armed with spontoons, who escorted the unit's flag) were easy to recognise due to the presence of a badge embroidered on top of their chevrons
- NCOs wore a red sash around the waist, which had a central band in the distinctive colour of each regiment
- Regiments having purple or red as their facing colour had the central band in white
- NCOs of the Highland regiments wore their sashes over the left shoulder
- The NCO sashes of rifle units were crimson with a central band in black.

Great Coat

During winter, especially on campaign, all ranks wore a great coat over their uniforms. This was of dark blue cloth for officers and dark grey for other ranks. It was double-breasted, with two rows of buttons on the front; the officers had a falling collar in the distinctive colour of their regiment. The officers of the rifle corps wore a great coat that was grey and had three rows of buttons on the front instead of two. It had dark green falling collar and cuffs. In December 1811, the colour of the officers' great coats was changed to dark grey for all units and a cape was added to protect the shoulders (it had been present on the great coat for other ranks since 1802). From 1806, badges of rank started to be worn on the right arm of great coats and the collars and cuffs of the great coats of NCOs were in regimental colour (like those of the officers).

Trousers and kilts

In 1793, all the British infantrymen (except the Highlanders) wore white breeches, which were used in combination with black woollen gaiters during winter and with white ones during summer. By July 1810, however, the white breeches were replaced by dark grey trousers that could be worn under or over the black woollen gaiters. During hot months, or when serving in tropical areas, white trousers and white gaiters were usually worn.

- The 5th Battalion of the 60th Regiment had dark blue trousers with red piping
- The 95th Rifles had dark green trousers
- The light regiments, created by converting line units, retained their previous breeches/trousers
- The Highland regiments wore their traditional Scottish kilts, each made with a distinctive weave of tartan cloth. On the front of their kilts the Highlanders wore the characteristic sporran and usually carried a 'sgian-dubh' (single-edged knife). Together with black shoes, the Highlanders also wore their traditional 'hose' (socks) that were made with white-and-red tartan for all regiments. During the Napoleonic Wars, for practical reasons, many Highlanders started to replace their kilts on campaign with trousers obtained from tartan cloth. These, known as 'trews', became extremely popular for everyday use and by 1815 most soldiers of the 93rd Foot had replaced their kilts with them.

Shoes and boots

NCOs and rankers of all units had black shoes, while officers used black leather boots.

Left: Front view of the personal equipment of an officer from a Highland regiment. (Photo and © Gordon's Living History)

Below left: Detail of a 'sporran' (pouch) used by an officer from a Highland regiment. (Photo and © Gordon's Living History)

Below middle: Detail of a Kilmarnock bonnet worn without feathers. (Photo and © Gordon's Living History)

Below right: Canteen used by the light company of the Gordon Highlanders. (Photo and © Gordon's Living History)

Belts and pouches

The standard set of personal equipment for a line infantryman comprised a white sling for the musket, a white crossbelt for the cartridge pouch, a white crossbelt for the bayonet scabbard, a black cartridge pouch, a black bayonet scabbard, a white canvas haversack, a wooden water bottle (usually painted pale blue) with dark brown sling and a canvas knapsack (which could be painted in different colours) and usually bore the unit number on the back. The knapsack had two white shoulder straps, connected on the chest by a horizontal belt of the same colour. Officers had a single white crossbelt for the sword. The rifle units (5th Battalion and rifle companies of the 60th and 95th Regiment) had the following black rather than white elements: carbine sling, crossbelt for the cartridge pouch, and straps of the knapsack. In addition, they used a black leather waistbelt which had a small pouch on the right side (used for transporting balls) and the bayonet scabbard on the left side. Very frequently, the riflemen also carried a white horn and a brown flask on their back, suspended by a dark green cord: the first was used to transport additional black powder, while the latter contained priming powder for the flintlock mechanism of their carbine.

Life Guards and Horse Guards uniforms

Pre-1797

The pre-1797 dress for the Life Guards was:

- black bicorn with yellow external edging, black cockade with yellow lace holder, white-and-red plume
- red coat with dark blue collar patches and round cuffs, dark blue frontal lapels, dark blue shoulder straps with yellow piping and fringes; additional stripes of yellow lace on the buttonholes of the collar patches (two), front of the coat (eight), cuffs (one) and sleeves (three); the buttonholes on the cuffs and sleeves were V-shaped. White turnbacks
- white trousers
- black leather tall boots
- white leather belt equipment.

The uniform of the Horse Guards was similar, but it had dark blue as main colour instead of red:

- black bicorn with yellow external edging, black cockade with yellow lace holder, white-and-red plume
- dark blue coat with red collar patches and round cuffs, red frontal lapels, red shoulder straps with yellow piping and fringes; additional stripes of yellow lace on the buttonholes of the collar patches (two), front of the coat (eight), cuffs (one) and sleeves (three); the buttonholes on the cuffs and sleeves were V-shaped. White turnbacks
- buff trousers
- black leather tall boots
- buff leather belt equipment.

During 1794 – for a brief period – the Blues wore a white metal cuirass over their uniforms, which was quite similar to that used by the contemporary French cuirassiers. This was used together with a buff leather waistbelt that had a black leather ammunition pouch on the front. Officers of both the Life Guards and the Horse Guards had all the yellow elements listed above in gold and wore a red sash wrapped around the waist; in addition, their rank was shown by golden epaulettes and contre-epaulettes that were worn on the shoulders instead of the shoulder straps.

1797 onwards

The M1797 dress was as follows for the Life Guards:

- black bicorn with yellow external edging, black cockade with yellow lace holder, white-and-red plume; red coat with dark blue collar and round cuffs, dark blue shoulder straps with yellow piping; additional stripes of yellow lace on the buttonholes of the collar (two), front of the coat (eight in four couples), cuffs (one) and sleeves (three); the buttonholes on the cuffs and sleeves were V-shaped. White turnbacks
- white trousers
- black leather tall boots and white leather belt equipment.

The uniform of the Horse Guards was similar to that described above, but it had dark blue as main colour instead of red:

- black bicorn with yellow external edging, black cockade with yellow lace holder, white-and-red plume
- dark blue coat with red collar and round cuffs, red shoulder straps with yellow piping; additional stripes of yellow lace on the buttonholes of the collar (two), front of the coat (eight in four couples), cuffs (one) and sleeves (three); the buttonholes on the cuffs and sleeves were V-shaped. White turnbacks
- buff trousers
- black leather tall boots and buff leather belt equipment.

1812 updates

The Life Guards and the Horse Guards adopted the new uniforms introduced for the line heavy cavalry in 1812 during 1813–14, after their deployment in the Iberian Peninsula. The shabraque used by both the Life Guards and the Horse Guards was dark blue with the royal monogram embroidered in gold on the back corner and on the pistols' holsters; on the external edge it had a golden band with red piping in the centre. The new **parade** dress comprised the following elements for the Life Guards:

- black leather helmet with brass frontal plate bearing the royal monogram on the front, brass peak, brass chinscale, brass crest covered with half-black and half-red fur (black in the top part, red in the bottom part), white-and-red plume (white in the top part, red in the bottom part like the previous one worn on the bicorn)
- red single-breasted jacket with dark blue collar and round cuffs both piped in yellow, yellow shoulder straps piped in dark blue, yellow piping to the front and bottom edges of the jacket, dark blue turnbacks piped in yellow (these were short and not long as in the previous dress)
- white trousers
- black leather boots and white leather belt equipment
- a red-and-yellow sash was worn around the waist.

This **campaign** dress was simpler with:

- the collar and cuffs of the jacket did not have yellow piping but additional yellow lace on the buttonholes
- around the waist, the piping to the front and bottom edges of the jacket was dark blue

- the shoulder straps were dark blue with red piping
- the white trousers were replaced by dark grey ones having a red double side-stripe.

The Horse Guards replaced their old uniform with bicorn and coat only around 1814, some months after the Life Guards; their new **parade** dress was as follows

- black leather helmet with brass frontal plate bearing the royal monogram on the front, brass peak, brass chinscale, brass crest covered with half-dark blue and half-red fur (dark blue in the top part, red in the bottom part), white-and-red plume (white in the top part, red in the bottom part like the previous one worn on the bicorn)
- dark blue single-breasted jacket with red collar and round cuffs both piped in yellow, red shoulder straps piped in yellow, yellow piping to the front and bottom edges of the jacket, red turnbacks piped in yellow (these were short and not long as in the previous dress)
- buff trousers
- black leather boots
- buff leather belt equipment
- a red-and-yellow sash was worn around the waist. A simpler dress was worn on *campaign*; this differed in some elements: the collar and cuffs of the jacket did not have yellow piping but additional yellow lace on the buttonholes; the piping to the front and bottom edges of the jacket was not yellow but white; the shoulder straps were dark blue with yellow piping
- the buff trousers were replaced by dark grey ones having red double side-stripe.

 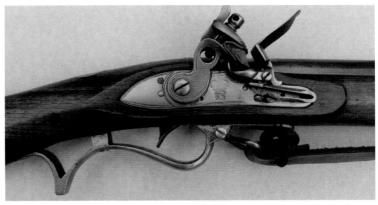

Above left: The M1812 shako worn by the 95th Rifles. (Photo and © 1/95th Rifles Living History Society)

Above right: Detail of a Baker carbine. (Photo and © 2nd Battalion, 95th Rifles)

Below: The Baker carbine used by the rifle units of the British infantry. (Photo and © 1/95th Rifles Living History Society)

Dragoon Guard and Dragoon uniforms

Until 1796, the British heavy cavalry continued to wear its pre-revolutionary uniforms, which comprised black bicorn hat and red tailcoat with open lapels in the distinctive colour of each regiment. In 1796, the lapels started to be worn buttoned up in order to form a single frontal plastron. In 1797, a new model of tailcoat was introduced. This was single-breasted and did not have lapels on the front and was much more comfortable to wear.

The pre-1797 dress was as follows:

- black bicorn with white-and-red plume and with black cockade having yellow lace holder; red coat with collar and round cuffs in regimental colour, frontal lapels in regimental colour, additional stripes of yellow lace on the buttonholes of the collar (one), front of the coat (eight in four pairs), cuffs (one) and sleeves (three); the buttonholes on the cuffs and sleeves were V-shaped. White turnbacks
- white trousers
- black leather tall boots
- white leather belt equipment

Officers had all the yellow elements listed above in gold and wore a red sash wrapped around the waist; in addition, their rank was shown by gold epaulettes and contre-epaulettes that were worn on the shoulders. The regimental colours, which did not change during the period were as follows:

Dark blue
1st Dragoon Guards, 1st, 2nd Dragoons, 3rd and 5th Dragoons.

Black
2nd and 7th Dragoon Guards

White
3rd and 6th Dragoon Guards

Medium blue
4th Dragoon Guards

Yellow
6th Dragoons

Light green
5th Dragoon Guards

Dark green
4th Dragoons

1797 uniforms

The new M1797 dress comprised the following elements

- black bicorn with black cockade having yellow lace holder and with white-and-red plume
- red coat with collar and round cuffs in regimental colour, shoulder straps in regimental colour with white or yellow piping, red shoulder wings piped in white or yellow; additional stripes of white or

yellow lace on the buttonholes of the collar (two), front of the coat (ten in five pairs), cuffs (one) and sleeves (one). Turnbacks in regimental colour
- white trousers
- black leather tall boots and white leather belt equipment.

Officers had all the white/yellow elements listed above in gold and wore a red sash wrapped around the waist; in addition, the shoulder straps and shoulder wings of their uniforms were covered with golden scales.

The **Scots Greys** was the only regiment that did not have the bicorn as headgear; instead men wore a black bearskin that was retained after the introduction of the new M1812 dress. This had a brass frontal plate reproducing the British coat of arms, a black leather peak, a white plume, brass chin scale and a decorative white cord with two tassels of the same colour. In addition, on the back, it was ornamented with a red circle inside which a white Horse of Hanover was embroidered. On campaign, the plume of the bearskin was removed and the whole headgear was protected by a cover made of oilskin. The piping colour of the various units could be white or yellow and helped to distinguish the corps with the same regimental colour, according to the following scheme:

Yellow
1st, 3rd, 5th and 7th Dragoon Guards. 1st Dragoons.

White
2nd, 4th, and 6th Dragoon Guards. 2nd, 4th, 5th and 6th Dragoons.

1812 uniforms
The new M1812 uniform comprised the following elements:

- black leather helmet with brass frontal plate bearing the royal monogram on the front, black leather peak, brass chin scale, brass crest covered with a black mane and having a black tuft on the front
- red single-breasted jacket with collar and pointed cuffs in regimental colour having white or yellow piping, shoulder straps in regimental colour having white or yellow piping, white or yellow piping to the front and bottom edges of the jacket, turnbacks in regimental colour with white or yellow piping (these were short unlike the previous dress)
- white trousers
- black leather boots
- white leather belt equipment.
- a sash was worn around the waist, which was in the regimental colour combined with the piping colour (white or yellow).

On **campaign**, the white trousers were replaced by dark grey ones with red piping and brown leather reinforcements on the inner thighs, both with parade dress and with campaign dress, wore the same uniforms as their men but with all the white/yellow elements in gold.

The 'shabraque' (saddlecloth) of most regiments was dark blue with the royal monogram embroidered in the piping colour of each unit on the back corner. In the external edge, it had a band in the piping colour of each unit with dark blue piping in the centre. Some regiments had the shabraque in regimental colour and not in dark blue. Over the shabraque, a protective black or white sheepskin was worn on most occasions.

The full personal equipment of a private from the 95th Rifles. (Photo and © 2nd Battalion, 95th Rifles)

Until 1812, **trumpeters** were dressed in the standard uniform of their regiment but with reversed colours. In that year, they received the same dress as the ordinary troopers but were easily distinguishable on the battlefield since the mane and the tuft of their helmets were red instead of black. In addition, they also had decorated shoulder wings.

Light Dragoon and Hussar uniforms

The British Light Dragoons used three different uniforms during the Napoleonic Period. The first was adopted in 1784, shortly after the end of the American Revolution, and consisted of a fur-crested Tarleton helmet worn with a short-tailed sleeved waistcoat and a sleeveless shell-jacket, both in dark blue. Until 1784, the Light Dragoons had been dressed in red like the rest of the British cavalry and the only specific item of uniform for the type was the black leather helmet (since the heavy cavalry had the more traditional bicorn as headgear). With the new dress regulations of 1784, however, it was decided to differentiate the Light Dragoons from the rest of the British cavalry. In 1796, this uniform was replaced with a new one, which was of clear hussar cut. The braided sleeved waistcoat was removed and the shell-jacket was modified to become a hussar's dolman, which had sleeves but not tails. The headgear remained the same, since the Tarleton helmet was extremely popular among ranks.

In 1807, some regiments of Light Dragoons were converted into hussar units and received new uniforms, which were extremely costly to produce but very elegant. These included dolman and pelisse in hussar-style and a busby covered with fur as headgear. The dolman and the pelisse both derived from the traditional dress of the Magyar hussars, since the first light cavalrymen of this specific troop type had appeared in Hungary during the previous centuries. The dolman was a jacket cut tight and short, decorated with multiple rows of buttons (usually three) and with some stripes of frogging on the front. The pelisse was a short fur-trimmed jacket worn loose over the left shoulder.

In 1812, the Light Dragoons received a new uniform, which remained in use until the end of the Napoleonic Wars. This included a black shako as headgear instead of the Tarleton helmet, and consisted of a dark blue tunic with coloured frontal plastron and short tails. The tunic of this M1812 dress was criticised by several British officers, including Wellington, because its colour and cut were too similar to those of the uniforms worn by the contemporary French cavalry. In particular, the new tunic looked very similar to the kurtka (short-tailed tunic with frontal plastron) of the Imperial Guard's Polish Lancers.

The M1784 uniform of the Light Dragoons was as follows:

- black leather Tarleton helmet with black peak, black fur crest, plume in regimental colour (worn on the left side), band wrapped around the bottom part in regimental colour, cockade on the back in regimental colour and white metal unit badge (worn on the right side)
- dark blue sleeveless shell jacket with collar in regimental colour piped in white, white frontal frogging and white piping to the front and bottom edges;
- dark blue short-tailed sleeved waistcoat with pointed cuffs in regimental colour piped in white, shoulder straps in regimental colour piped in white, additional white braiding on the buttonholes of the waistcoat's front
- white trousers
- black leather boots
- white belt equipment.

The officers wore the same uniform described above, but with all the white elements in silver. In addition, they had a red sash worn around the waist, and instead of the shoulder straps they had shoulder wings covered with silver scales.

The regiments of Light Dragoons that were raised for service in India wore a version of this same dress

- black leather Tarleton helmet with black peak, black fur crest, plume in regimental colour (worn on the left side), band wrapped around the bottom part in regimental colour, cockade on the back in regimental colour and white metal unit badge (worn on the right side)

- light blue-grey sleeveless shell jacket with collar in regimental colour piped in white, white frontal frogging and white piping to the front and bottom edges
- light blue-grey short-tailed sleeved waistcoat with pointed cuffs in regimental colour piped in white, shoulder straps in regimental colour piped in white, additional white braiding on the buttonholes of the waistcoat's front
- white trousers
- black leather short boots
- white leather belt equipment.

1796 uniform

The M1796 uniform of the Light Dragoons comprised the following elements:

- black leather Tarleton helmet with black peak, black fur crest, plume in regimental colour (worn on the left side), band wrapped around the bottom part in regimental colour, cockade on the back in regimental colour and white metal unit badge (worn on the right side)
- dark blue dolman with collar and pointed cuffs in regimental colour, both piped in white; shoulder wings in regimental colour with white piping, white frontal frogging with three rows of vertical buttons, white decorative Hungarian knots embroidered on the pointed cuffs and front of the trousers
- dark blue trousers
- black leather short boots with frontal tassel
- white leather belt equipment.
- a sabretache (small bag), which was part of the contemporary hussar dress and which was used to transport documents.

The officers wore the same uniform described above, but with all the white elements in silver; in addition, they had a red sash worn around the waist and their Hungarian knots (embroidered on the cuffs and trousers) were more complex according to their rank.

The regiments of Light Dragoons serving in India wore a peculiar version of this same dress:

- black leather Tarleton helmet with black peak, black fur crest, plume in regimental colour (worn on the left side), band wrapped around the bottom part in regimental colour, cockade on the back in regimental colour and white metal unit badge (worn on the right side)
- light blue-grey dolman with collar and pointed cuffs in regimental colour, both piped in white; shoulder wings in regimental colour with white piping, white frontal frogging with three rows of vertical buttons, white decorative Hungarian knots embroidered on the pointed cuffs and front of the trousers
- light blue-grey trousers
- black leather short boots with frontal tassel
- white leather belt equipment.

1807 uniform

The M1807 uniform adopted by those regiments that were converted into hussar units was as follows:

- tall busby covered with brown fur having white cords, white-and-red short plume and red soft bag on the right side.

- Dark blue dolman with collar and cuffs in regimental colour, both piped in white; white frontal frogging with three rows of buttons, white piping to front and bottom edges, white Hungarian knots embroidered on the sleeves
- dark blue pelisse lined with fur, having white frontal frogging and white piping to the cuffs; around the waist there was a wrapped sash, in two different colours that varied for each regiment
- white trousers
- black leather short boots with frontal tassel
- white leather belt equipment
- the sabretache bag, but the hussar's model was not entirely black like that of the Light Dragoons but was decorated with ornate embroidery that reproduced the unit badge of each regiment.

Officers were dressed like their men, but the white elements of the latter's dress were all silver. In addition, the cords of the busby were gold rather than white.

In 1812, a new model of busby was introduced, which was gradually adopted by all the hussar regiments by 1815; this was shorter but larger when compared with the previous one; in addition, it had yellow cords instead of white ones and a brass chin scale.

1812 uniform

The M1812 uniform of the Light Dragoons comprised the following elements:

- black shako with white/yellow top band, white/yellow frontal pompom, white-and-red short plume, white/yellow cords, black leather peak, brass chin scale, black cockade with white/yellow external edge
- dark blue tunic with collar and pointed cuffs in regimental colour, frontal plastron in regimental colour, white epaulettes on the shoulders, piping to the rear seams of the tunic in regimental colour, short turnbacks in regimental colour, dark blue pockets piped in regimental colour on the back of the turnbacks; around the waist was wrapped a sash, in dark blue and in regimental colour
- grey trousers with red double side-stripe. On campaign, the trousers had a black or brown leather reinforcement on the internal part
- black leather short boots
- black leather sabretache
- white leather belt equipment.

Officers were dressed similarly to their men, but with several elements of their uniform in gold:

- black shako with golden top band, golden frontal pompom, white-and-red short plume, golden cords, black leather peak, brass chin scale, black cockade with golden external edge
- dark blue tunic with collar and pointed cuffs in regimental colour, frontal plastron in regimental colour, golden epaulettes on the shoulders, piping to the rear seams of the tunic in regimental colour, short turnbacks in regimental colour, dark blue pockets piped in regimental colour on the back of the turnbacks
- around the waist was wrapped a sash, in gold and in regimental colour
- grey trousers with golden single side-stripe
- black leather short boot
- black leather sabretache
- white leather belt equipment.

Ammunition pouch and sword-bayonet used by the 95th Rifles. (Photo and © 2nd Battalion, 95th Rifles)

The regimental colours of the Light Dragoons units, which did not change during the period, were:

White
7th, 17th, 18th, 24th, and 27th Regiment of Light Dragoons

Scarlet red
8th, 15th, 16th, and 22nd Regiment of Light Dragoons

Yellow
10th, 19th, 20th, 28th, and 31st Regiment of Light Dragoons

Pale yellow
12th Regiment of Light Dragoons

Lemon-yellow
14th Regiment of Light Dragoons

Blue
23rd, 26th, 30th, 32nd, and 33rd Regiment of Light Dragoons

Buff
25th, and 29th Regiment of Light Dragoons

Pale buff
9th, 11th and 13th Regiment of Light Dragoons

Until 1812, the shabraque of the Light Dragoons was in regimental colour, with the royal monogram embroidered in a countering colour on the back corner and on the pistol's holsters; on the external edge it had a band in countering colour with a line of piping in the centre.

In 1812, a new shabraque was introduced: this was dark blue with the royal monogram embroidered in regimental colour on the back corner; on the external edge it had a band in regimental colour. Over the new shabraque a protective black or white sheepskin was worn on most occasions. Hussar regiments had a different model of shabraque, dark blue with the royal monogram embroidered on the back corner and with an indented band in regimental colour on the external edge. It was used in combination with a protective black or white sheepskin. Until 1812, the trumpeters of the Light Dragoons were dressed with the standard uniform of their regiment but with reversed colours; in that year they received the same dress as the ordinary troopers but were easily distinguishable on the battlefield since the plume of their shakos was entirely red.

Ammunition pouch and sword-bayonet used by the 95th Rifles. (Photo and © 2nd Battalion, 95th Rifles)

Artillery and Specialist Corps uniforms

Royal Artillery
The uniforms of the Royal Artillery and of the smaller technical corps were very similar to those of the British line infantry or light cavalry. The Foot Artillery, Royal Engineers, Royal Sappers and Royal Staff Corps were dressed similarly to the line infantry. The Horse Artillery, Rocket Troops, Royal Artillery Drivers and Royal Waggon Train were uniformed similarly to the light cavalry. In 1793, the Foot Artillery was dressed with long-tail coats, which were worn open from the neck and sloped away at the waist. The main colour was dark blue (the distinctive colour of the Royal Artillery), with collar and cuffs in red. The lapels were red, while the turn-backs were white. The skirt and linings over which the coat was worn were white. The dark blue coat had horizontal pockets and could be worn with the lapels buttoned over or folded back. All the buttonholes of the coat (on collar, cuffs and frontal lapels) had some additional yellow lace. The headgear was a black bicorn with yellow external edging, black cockade and white plume.

In 1796, the coat design, which had not changed since the American Revolution, was to be more practical and modern. Now it was to be fastened to the waist; the lapels were retained (for the moment) but were made to button over. The collar was now a standing one.

In October 1797, the lapels were removed for all non-officers and the dark blue coat of the British Foot Artillery became a single-breasted jacket with false tails) and started to have vertical pockets on the back. On the front, the new jacket had a single line of buttons and was decorated with yellow lace embroidered under the buttons and on the buttonholes. The main colour of the uniform remained dark blue; collar and round cuffs were red, piped in yellow. The jacket had red shoulder straps piped in yellow as pre-1796 uniform, but now with a yellow crest where they were sewn to the shoulder and were pointed at the other end (where they were secured, close to the collar, by a small button). With the new uniform, grey trousers were worn during winter and white ones for summer.

In 1800, the bicorn was replaced by the shako. The M1800 shako was made of black felt and had a flat peak on the front; the crown had a cylindrical shape. On the top of the crown was a worsted wool tuft in white; at the base of the tuft was a black cockade, which carried a small button at its centre. The front of the shako carried a large plate made of tin, having a specific design die-stamped on the rear that reproduced the Royal Artillery's coat of arms.

During 1812, a new model of shako was introduced, which was more comfortable and more practical to wear on the battlefield. This became known as Belgian or Waterloo shako, since it was used on a large scale during the Belgian campaign of 1815. The main feature of this new headgear was that it had a crown that sloped down at the back, producing a false front. On the rear, the crown was also broader. Like the previous shako it was made of black felt. The false front was edged with black lace and on the front of the headgear there was a peak made of lacquered leather. The M1812 shako had a white worsted tuft on the left side, at the base of which there was the usual black cockade, held in place by a button. On the front of the shako there was a yellow twist cord with a tassel at each end; a doubled loop knot was formed to shorten the cord into two lengths of chain with an un-knotted length at the centre. The cord was worn with the doubled loop end hooked behind the cockade, with the two lengths of loop knots each side of the shako plate and the two tassels on the right. The frontal plate of the M1812 shako was made of brass and reproduced a design that was specific to the Royal Artillery.

Until 1797, the officers of the Foot Artillery dressed like the rank and file, but with some differences: the external edging of their bicorn was golden, they had golden epaulettes on the shoulders and wore a red sash around the waist.

With the adoption of the new M1797 dress, the officers of the Foot Artillery started to be uniformed as follows:

- black bicorn with white plume and black cockade
- dark blue double-breasted tunic with red standing collar and round cuffs, golden epaulettes showing rank on the shoulders
- red sash worn around the waist
- white trousers
- black leather boots.
- belt equipment was white leather both for officers and rankers.

Royal Engineers

Until 1797, the officers of the Royal Engineers were dressed like those of the Foot Artillery, but the facing colour of their uniform was black instead of red; in addition, they did not have additional yellow lace on the buttonholes of their tunic.

1797 Uniform

The new uniform adopted since 1797 was as follows:

- black bicorn with white plume and black cockade
- dark blue double-breasted tunic with black standing collar and round cuffs, golden epaulettes showing rank on the shoulders
- red sash worn around the waist
- white trousers
- black leather boots.

Royal Military Artificers

Until 1797, the Royal Military Artificers wore the following dress:

- black round hat with yellow bottom band and red plume applied over a black cockade
- dark blue long-tailed coat with black standing collar and round cuffs, black frontal lapels, additional yellow lace on the buttonholes of the coat (on collar, cuffs and lapels)
- white waistcoat and trousers
- white leather belt equipment.

On active service the plume of the hat and the frontal lapels of the coat were usually removed.

1797 uniform

In 1797, the following new uniform came into use:

- black 'stovepipe' shako with white plume, black cockade and brass frontal plate
- dark blue single-breasted jacket with black standing collar piped in yellow and black round cuffs, black shoulder straps piped in yellow, additional yellow lace on the buttonholes of the jacket (on the front and on the cuffs)
- white trousers
- black gaiters.

1812 uniform as Royal Sappers and Miners

When the Royal Military Artificers were reorganised as the Royal Sappers and Miners in 1812, they received the following new dress:

- black 'Belgian' shako with white plume, yellow cords, black cockade and brass frontal plat
- red single-breasted jacket with dark blue standing collar piped in yellow and dark blue round cuffs, dark blue shoulder straps piped in yellow, additional yellow lace on the buttonholes of the jacket (on the front and on the cuffs)
- grey trousers
- black gaiters.

On active service, a simpler version of the jacket was worn, which did not have additional yellow lace on the buttonholes and piping to collar/shoulder straps. An undress cap made of black leather was also used, which had the brass initials 'RS & M' on the front.

1812 amalgamated regiment uniform

In 1812, following their integration with the Royal Sappers and Miners, also the Royal Engineers received a new red uniform:

- black bicorn with white plume and black cockade
- red double-breasted tunic with dark blue standing collar and round cuffs, additional golden lace on the buttonholes of the collar and cuffs, golden epaulettes showing rank on the shoulders
- red sash worn around the waist
- grey trousers with red side-stripe
- black leather boots.

Royal Staff Corp

The soldiers of the Royal Staff Corps were dressed as follows since 1800:

- black shako with brass frontal plate, black cockade and white-and-red plume
- red single-breasted jacket with dark blue standing collar and round cuffs, white piping to collar and cuffs, dark blue shoulder straps piped in white
- dark blue trousers
- black leather short boots
- white leather belt equipment.

Horse Artillery

Until 1799, the troopers of the Horse Artillery were dressed very similarly to the Light Dragoons, but the piping colour of their uniform was yellow and not white:

- black leather Tarleton helmet with black peak, black fur crest, white plume (worn on the left side), black band with yellow stripes wrapped around the bottom part, black cockade on the back, brass chin scale and brass unit badge representing a flaming grenade (worn on the right side)
- dark blue sleeveless shell jacket with red collar piped in yellow, yellow frontal frogging and yellow piping to the front and bottom edges
- dark blue short-tailed sleeved waistcoat with red pointed cuffs piped in yellow, red shoulder straps piped in yellow, additional yellow braiding on the buttonholes of the waistcoat's front
- white trousers
- black leather boots
- white belt equipment.

1799 uniform

In 1799, the following new uniform was introduced, which was retained in service until the end of the Napoleonic Wars:

- black leather Tarleton helmet with black peak, black fur crest, white plume (worn on the left side), black band with yellow stripes wrapped around the bottom part, brass chin scale and brass unit badge representing a flaming grenade (worn on the right side)

- dark blue dolman with red collar and pointed cuffs piped in yellow, yellow piping to the bottom edge and to the rear seams, yellow frontal frogging with three vertical rows of buttons
- grey trousers with red side-stripe and brown leather reinforcement on the internal part
- black leather short boots
- white leather belt equipment.

Rocket Troops

The Rocket Troops organised in 1813 were uniformed exactly like the Horse Artillery, of which they were part.

Royal Artillery Drivers

The Royal Artillery Drivers were initially dressed with a very simple uniform, of clear civilian cut:

- black leather undress cap with the brass initials 'C R A D' (Corps of the Royal Artillery Drivers) on the front
- dark blue single-breasted jacket with red collar and round cuffs, three rows of vertical buttons on the front
- white trousers
- black leather boots.

1811 uniform

Around 1811, this was progressively substituted by a new dress, which was as follows:

- black leather Tarleton helmet with black peak, black fur crest, white plume (worn on the left side), dark blue band with yellow stripes wrapped around the bottom part, brass chin scale and brass unit badge representing the shield of the Artillery Ordnance (worn on the right side
- dark blue single-breasted jacket with three vertical rows of buttons on the front having double yellow piping, red collar and pointed cuffs piped in yellow, grey trousers with red side-stripe and brown leather reinforcement on the internal part
- black leather short boots
- white leather belt equipment.

Royal Waggon Train

Until 1811, the Royal Waggon Train wore the same uniform of the Royal Artillery Drivers, but with different brass initials on the black leather undress cap. In 1811, the following new dress was adopted, which was similar to that worn by the Royal Artillery Drivers but was red instead of dark blue and had a different headgear:

- black shako with white top band, white pompom, white-and-red short plume, white cords, black leather peak, white metal chin scale, black cockade with white external edge
- red single-breasted jacket with three vertical rows of buttons on the front having double white piping, dark blue collar and pointed cuffs piped in white
- grey trousers with dark blue side-stripe and brown leather reinforcement on the internal part
- black leather short boots
- white leather belt equipment.

Staff Corps of Cavalry

Initially the members of the Staff Corps of Cavalry retained the uniforms of their former regiments and simply wore a red scarf tied around their right shoulder as a mark of distinction; very soon, however, they received a red uniform that was very similar to that worn by the Light Dragoons:

- black shako with white top band, white pompom, red short plume, white cords, black leather peak, white metal chin scale, black cockade with white external edge
- red tunic with dark blue collar and pointed cuffs piped in white, dark blue frontal plastron piped in white, dark blue shoulder straps piped in white, white piping to the rear seams of the tunic, dark blue short turnbacks, red pockets piped in dark blue on the back of the turnbacks
- red-and-dark blue sash wrapped around the waist
- grey trousers with dark blue double side-stripe
- black leather short boots
- black leather sabretache
- white leather belt equipment.

Royal Marines

The Royal Marines were always dressed in red like the line infantry of the British Army; as a result, they were given the nickname of 'Lobsters' from the sailors who served with them on the warships of the Royal Navy. The uniform worn until 1802 was as follows:

- black bicorn with white external edge and black cockade
- red long-tailed coat with white collar and round cuffs, white shoulder straps, white frontal lapels
- white waistcoat and trousers
- black gaiters
- white leather belt equipment.

1802 uniform

In 1802, a new dress was adopted, which remained unchanged until the end of the Napoleonic Wars:

- black round hat with white band wrapped around the bottom part and white-and-red plum
- red single-breasted jacket with dark blue collar and round cuffs, white piping to collar, additional white lace on the buttonholes of the jacket's front and of the cuffs, dark blue shoulder straps with white piping and white crest,
- white trousers
- black gaiter
- white leather belt equipment.

Royal Marine Artillery

The Royal Marine Artillery was dressed very similarly to the Foot Artillery:

- black round hat with brass frontal plate, black cockade and white plume
- dark blue single-breasted jacket with red collar and round cuffs piped in yellow, red shoulder straps piped in yellow, additional yellow lace on the buttonholes of the jacket's front and cuffs
- dark blue trousers

Ammunition pouch of the 95th Rifles. (Photo and © 2nd Battalion, 95th Rifles)

- black gaiters
- white leather belt equipment.

On campaign the round cap was replaced by a dark blue fatigue cap and a simpler version of the jacket (without piping and additional lace on the buttonholes) was worn.

Foreign troops and King's German Legion

King's Dutch Brigade
The line infantry was dressed like its British equivalent but with reversed colours (dark blue jacket with red facings) and grey trousers. The jagers wore dark green jacket with black facings (including frontal plastron) and grey trousers.

Dutch Light Infantry Battalion

- black shako
- dark blue single-breasted jacket with orange facings
- grey trousers

Dillon's Regiment
It wore the same uniform of the line infantry, with yellow facings.

Chasseurs Britanniques
It wore the same uniform of the line infantry, with sky blue facings.

Maltese Provincial Battalions
It wore the same uniform of the line infantry, with sky blue facings for 1st Battalion and green ones for 2nd Battalion.

Royal Regiment of Malta
It wore the same uniform of the line infantry, with dark blue facings.

Royal Corsican Rangers
It wore the same uniform of the 60th Foot's 5th Battalion.

Royal Sicilian Regiment
It wore the same uniform of the line infantry (green facings) but with Tarleton helmet having green plume.

Calabrian Free Corps
The first uniform of this corps comprised:

- black slouch hat (with the left part of the brim turned up) having a green plume and a yellow band wrapped around the bottom part
- dark blue single-breasted jacket with five rows of buttons on the front, yellow collar and cuffs decorated with dark blue embroidering
- dark green trousers

In 1813, a new dress was introduced:

- black shako with dark green frontal plume
- dark blue single-breasted jacket with frontal plastron piped in yellow and edged by a line of buttons shaped like a U, yellow collar and round cuffs
- dark blue trousers

Italian Levy

- black shako
- dark blue single-breasted jacket with red collar and round cuffs, red piping to front of the jacket and short turnbacks
- grey trousers

Piedmontese Legion

- black shako
- dark blue single-breasted jacket with red collar and round cuffs, red piping to front of the jacket and short turnbacks
- dark blue trousers

Ionian Islands Volunteer Militia

No uniform, Greek civilian clothing.

Greek Light Infantry Regiments

- red skull cap with tassel in regimental colour
- red oriental-style jacket with cuffs and decorative trim in regimental colour
- red shirt with decorative trim in regimental colour
- entirely white fustanella (kilt)
- white breeches
- red socks

The regimental colour was yellow for the 1st Regiment and green for the 2nd Regiment. The officers had a black neo-classical helmet as headgear and the decorative trim of their jacket/shirt was golden. They also wore red greaves (decorated with gold) over the lower legs and knee-protectors decorated with golden lion's heads.

Meuron Regiment
Same uniform of the line infantry, with sky blue facings.

Roll Regiment
Same uniform of the line infantry, with sky blue facings.

Watteville Regiment
Same uniform of the line infantry, with black facings.

KGL line infantry
Same uniform of the British line infantry, with dark blue facings.

KGL light infantry
Same uniform of the 95th Rifles, but with a single row of buttons on the front of the jacket and grey trousers.

KGL heavy cavalry
Same uniform of the British heavy cavalry.

KGL light cavalry
Same uniform of the British light cavalry.

Powder flask of the 95th Rifles. (Photo and © 2nd Battalion, 95th Rifles)

Bibliography

Barnes RM, *A History of the Regiments and Uniforms of the British Army*, Seeley Service, 1950

Chappell M, *Redcaps: Britain's Military Police*, Osprey Publishing, 1997

Chappell M, *The King's German Legion 1803–1812*, Osprey Publishing, 2000

Chappell M, *The King's German Legion 1812–1816*, Osprey Publishing, 2000

Chappell M, *Wellington's Peninsula Regiments: The Irish*, Osprey Publishing, 2003

Chappell M., *Wellington's Peninsula Regiments: The Light Infantry*, Osprey Publishing, 2004

Chartrand R, *A Scarlet Coat: Uniforms, Flags and Equipment of the British Forces in the War of 1812*, Service Publications, 2011

Chartrand R, *British Forces in North America 1793–1815*, Osprey Publishing, 1998

Chartrand R, *British Forces in the West Indies 1793–1815*, Osprey Publishing, 1996

Chartrand R, *Emigré and Foreign Troops in British Service 1793–1803*, Osprey Publishing, 1999

Chartrand R, *Emigré and Foreign Troops in British Service 1803–1815*, Osprey Publishing, 2000

Esposito G, *Armies of the War of 1812: United States, United Kingdom and Canada 1812–1815*, Winged Hussar Publishing, 2017

Fletcher I, *Wellington's Foot Guards*, Osprey Publishing, 1994

Fosten B, *Wellington's Heavy Cavalry*, Osprey Publishing, 1982

Fosten B, *Wellington's Infantry (1)*, Osprey Publishing, 1981

Fosten B, *Wellington's Infantry (2)*, Osprey Publishing, 1982

Fosten B, *Wellington's Light Cavalry*, Osprey Publishing, 1982

Franklin CE, *British Napoleonic Uniforms*, The History Press, 2008

Fraser D, *The Grenadier Guards*, Osprey Publishing, 1978

Funcken F and Funcken L, *British Infantry Uniforms: from Malborough to Wellington*, Littlehampton Book Services, 1977

Grant C, *The Coldstream Guards*, Osprey Publishing, 1971

Haythornthwaite P, *British Cavalryman 1792-1815*, Osprey Publishing, 1994

Haythornthwaite P, *British Rifleman 1797–1815*, Osprey Publishing, 2002

Haythornthwaite P, *Nelson's Navy*, Osprey Publishing, 1993

Haythornthwaite P, *The Armies of Wellington*, Arms and Armour Press, 1994

Haythornthwaite P, *Uniforms of the Peninsular War 1807–1814*, Blandford Press, 1978

Haythornthwaite P, *Uniforms of Waterloo in Colour*, Blandford Press, 1974

Haythornthwaite P, *Wellington's Army: the Uniforms of the British Soldier 1812–1815*, Greenhill Books, 2002

Haythornthwaite P, *Wellington's Specialist Troops*, Osprey Publishing, 1988

Hofschroer P, *The Hanoverian Army of the Napoleonic Wars*, Osprey Publishing, 1989

Katcher P, *The American War 1812-1814*, Osprey Publishing, 1990

Lawson Cecil CP, *A History of the Uniforms of the British Army*, Littlehampton Book Services, 1974

Reid S, *Armies of the East India Company 1750–1850*, Osprey Publishing, 2009

Reid S, *British Redcoat 1793–1815*, Osprey Publishing, 1997

Reid S, *Wellington's Highlanders*, Osprey Publishing, 1992

Windrow M, *Military Dress of the Peninsular War 1808–1814*, Hippocrene Books, 1975

The Re-enactors

1/95th Rifles Living History Society

Our Society consists of people from all walks of life, coming together to share a passion for recreating a part of our military heritage. We enjoy and take pride in what we do, entertaining and enlightening members of the public about this period in history through our shows and events. We are a family-orientated unit with partners and children welcomed. Annually, between March and October, we take part in events such as battle re-enactments, training and drill, parades and proms. As a 'living history' society we usually set up a period encampment consisting of period canvas tents, equipment, cooking methods and utensils that assist us in 'living' and depicting the way of life. 95th Rifles Living History Society foundations were established in 1973 as an experimental group of riflemen re-enactors and developed into its present format in 1975. The Society has developed steadily into one of the finest and most respected Napoleonic re-enactment groups at home and abroad. We are not limited to just one regiment and, indeed, one representative country. The Society is composed of two brother regiments that are an integral part of its structure – the British 95th (Rifle) Regiment of Foot and the French 62eme Regiment d'Infanterie de Ligne. As one of the founding members of the Napoleonic Association, representing the 1st Battalion, 95th (Rifle) Regiment of Foot, we take part in events and shows across the UK and Europe.

Contact
Email: webmaster@1st95thrifles.com
Website: www.1st95thrifles.com/
Facebook: facebook.com/195thRiflesLivingHistorySociety

23rd Regiment of Foot, The Royal Welch Fusiliers 1809–1815

'I saw the 23rd the other day and I never saw a regiment in such order. They are not strong in numbers, but it was the most complete and handsome military body I ever looked at.'

Duke of Wellington

Over the hills of Portugal and Spain, through blood-soaked Albuera to the killing fields of Waterloo, this regiment of astonishing infantry marched with Wellington to defeat the forces of Bonaparte. The 're-created' regiment now carry its colours, fight battles, and live in the manner of its forebears. Our period camp is the centre of a well ordered military day, and – of course – a convivial evening. We attend events large and small, locally and overseas. We are a group of red-coat re-enactors based mainly along the Welsh Borders and the West Country. The group was first formed in 1995 by like-minded individuals who wanted to recreate one of the finest Welsh infantry regiments that took part in defeating the 'Corsican ogre', as the French emperor Napoleon Bonaparte was called. The 23rd mainly attend events in the UK, but can regularly be seen taking part in battle re-enactments in France, Belgium, The Netherlands, Portugal and Spain. In our regiment we have roles for everyone and more than enough equipment to loan any new recruit.

Contact
Website: www.23rdrwf.com/
Facebook: www.facebook.com/23rdrwf

2nd Battalion, 95th Rifles

Since formation in 1998, our aim has been to represent the riflemen of Wellington's army just as they would have been while on active service during the Peninsular War (1808–14) and the Waterloo Campaign of 1815. We are a very welcoming unit, with membership coming from across Britain and containing a good mix of age groups and backgrounds. Our events often take us to picturesque, historic and unique locations across the country, as well as to Europe. Our uniforms and equipment are based on examination of original examples, research into the uniform regulations and study of contemporary images in order to create as accurate an image as possible. Our drill and tactics are taken from extensive research into, and experimentation with, the drill manuals of the time. We are a very active group, working to maintain our standards and constantly seeking to improve our impression. Living history is a very important part of our unit as a soldier could spend more time in the camp than on the battlefield. It also gives the women and children of the unit a chance to recreate the way of life for a family of a Napoleonic soldier. Our meals are based upon period recipes and cooked over an open fire, which becomes the heart of the camp.

Contact
Email: events@95th-rifles.co.uk
Website: www.95th-rifles.co.uk/
Facebook: www.facebook.com/2ndBn95thRifles/?ref=page_internal

32nd Cornwall Regiment of Foot

The 32nd Regiment of Foot (Cornwall) is a re-enactment group based in Cornwall and Devon, and is part of the Napoleonic Association. Our group strives to open the world of living history to everyone. We aim to portray all aspects of life in the Regiment, and welcome camp followers, traders, surgeons… anyone who would like to take part in living history. We also welcome people interested in researching and re-creating the period. Our creative contacts produce high quality reproductions of the clothing, uniforms and equipment of the Napoleonic era. At our events, you can experience dramatic gun-firing exhibitions, military marching and drill displays, either as a single regiment or part of a much larger battalion. We camp under canvas, cook over an open fire and march to the beat of our own fife and drum. We are frequently invited to living history events and large-scale battle re-enactments in the UK and abroad. The original 32nd Regiment achieved great triumphs and suffered great loss, but is not among the most famous of the regiments who took part in the Napoleonic Wars – something we hope to change. We try and recreate the regiment as it was between 1808 and 1815 by showing the social life in camp and the military life in battle. We have come together through many different interests; from military history, Regency life-style, model-making to historic firearms.

Contact
Email: nigewren@gmail.com
Website: www.32ndcornwallregiment.co.uk
Facebook: www.facebook.com/32ndRegiment

44th East Essex Regiment of Foot

We are a living history and re-enactment group, representing one of the famous British Army regiments of the early 19th century – The 44th East Essex. The 44th has a long history stretching back to 1748 and through subsequent changes and amalgamations. Its roots are embodied in the current Royal Anglian Regiment. We are the 2nd Battalion, whose reputation for skill and courage throughout these European wars was second to none – with particular mention made of their service at the siege of Badajoz (1812) and the capture of the Eagle of the 62eme at Salamanca (1812). The unit served with great distinction and suffered heavy casualties at Quatre Bras (1815) and as part of Sir Dennis Pack's 9th Brigade at Waterloo. Occasional excursions to Canada and the US, to join events linked to the War of 1812 and the conclusion of these wars at New Orleans in late 1814/early 1815, has necessitated portraying the 1st Battalion on such occasions. The 44th Regiment of Foot (East Essex) takes part regularly in displays, living history and battle re-enactments at home and across Europe. The Regiment is affiliated to the Napoleonic Association of Great Britain and forms a fundamental part of the Allied army when in action overseas.

Contact
Email: 44threcruitingparty@gmail.com
Website: www.44theastessex.com/
Facebook: www.facebook.com/44theastessex

Gordon's Living History

Gordon's Living History is a re-enactment group based in the Netherlands. It portrays the Scottish regiment The Gordon Highlanders through the ages. Our aim is to portray the regiment as accurately as we can and to have a lot of fun doing so. Our primary focus is the regiment during the Napoleonic wars. We portray the Light Company of the 92nd Regiment of Foot (The Gordon Highlanders), the official name of the regiment at that time. We often work together with our sister unit based in Germany, which portrays the Grenadier Company. We show the military side, as well as the civilians who would have been in the camp and followed the army. A number of our members have the uniform and equipment that the regiment wore and used during the 2nd Boer War in South Africa (1899–1902). Some of our female members portray the British nurses that were sent to South Africa to take care of the wounded. We portray this period less frequently, due mainly to the limited amount of events. World War One or Great War is also one of our focus periods. As Gordon's Living History, we try to present an accurate impression of how a rifleman looked and the kind of equipment he would have had. The equipment of the soldiers changed during the war and we try to show these changes in our uniform. For World War Two, we portray the 1st Battalion Gordon Highlanders, which was part of the 51st Highland Division.

Contact
E-mail: bestuur.92ndgordons@gmail.com
Website: https://www.gordonslivinghistory.nl/
Facebook: https://www.facebook.com/GordonsLivingHistory

His Majesty's 33rd Regiment of Foot

The 33rd Foot is modelled on a standard battalion company of a line regiment of infantry during the period 1812–16. We represent an ordinary company of red-coated line infantry. Emphasis is placed on the life of the ordinary rank and file – the private soldier – that made up the backbone of the army. As a company, we attend events all over the country ranging from small appearances to large battles with hundreds involved. Larger events often occur on the continent with many nationalities taking part. There are also many 'living history' events where we show how soldiers lived from day to day. Barracks' scenes and camps are often set up showing many of the other activities soldiers took part in when not fighting. During the winter months, we have regular meetings and drill practice where members learn the required drill and manoeuvres. Many of our members are keen military historians and a great deal of research into the period is conducted. Known alternatively as The 1st Yorkshire West Riding Regiment our headquarters is in Halifax and most members come from the north of England. The regiment still exists as the 3rd Battalion of the Yorkshire Regiment, with whom we have links through its regimental museum in Halifax. The 33rd played a major part at Waterloo: standing in the frontline at the centre of the ridge the unit suffered almost 50 per cent casualties. Richard Sharpe, made famous by Sean Bean in the long-running TV series and popular books, 'served' in the 33rd.

Contact
Website: http://33rdfoot.co.uk/
Facebook: https://www.facebook.com/the33rdFoot

King's German Legion Artillery

The King's German Artillery is a living history and re-enactment unit, which recreates the splendour, drama and camaraderie of the Napoleonic era through the lens of the King's German Legion 4th Foot Artillery Battery. Our unit has five cannons of various sizes, all capable of being fired with real gunpowder as well as enthusiasm. We use uniforms, equipment and techniques authentic to the period of the Napoleonic Wars to create spectacles for any audience. We attend events as members of the Napoleonic Association (link), as well as numerous private events throughout the year. Typically spanning an entire weekend, we will set up camp, and dig in for two days of living as soldiers of the British Army might have done 200 years ago. There will usually be multiple set-piece battles over the course of the weekend, in which we join with infantry and cavalry units to do battle against the French. The rest of the time is mostly spent in and around the camp, providing entertainment and education for members of the public. We take advantage of any opportunity to teach people the workings of a field cannon, and to demonstrate the various tasks that formed part of camp life for soldiers. Once the sun goes down, the King's German Legion Artillery comes into its own. We pride ourselves on being the loudest both on and off the battlefield. The King's German Legion was famed for its music-making and we delight in carrying on this tradition, with a wide repertoire of sea shanties and folk songs that can be heard at full volume late into the night.

Contact
Email: kga@kingsgermanartillery.uk
Website: https://kingsgermanartillery.uk/
Facebook: https://www.facebook.com/KGAUK

Old 68th Society

The 68th Society was created in 1975 to keep alive the memory of the Durham Light Infantry, one of the most famous county regiments. We do this through our mission to interpret the regiment, and more generally the ordinary British soldier, from 1758 through to World War Two. The 68th is dedicated to the attaining highest levels of historical accuracy and interpretation. We work together to further this work through research, recreating high quality replicas and providing public display across the UK and Europe.

Contact
Email: old_68th@outlook.com
Website: https://www.68dli.co.uk/index.php
Facebook: https://www.facebook.com/68thsociety

The 79th Cameron Highlanders

We are a group of like-minded people who are interested in history and re-enact life as it would have been in the 79th Cameron Highlanders Regiment during the Peninsular Wars and up to the Battle of Waterloo in 1815. We try to recreate, as authentically as possible, the everyday life for the soldiers and their families within the regiment, using costume, muskets, drill and food cooked to authentic recipes and day-to-day routine life in the camp. The regiment regularly meets at Fort Amherst, Chatham, Kent. A Napoleonic Fort, which is one of the best preserved Napoleonic fortresses in England; it was designed and built to protect Chatham Dockyard situated on the banks of the river Medway during the time of threat and invasion by our enemies. It is also where Nelson's famous flagship HMS *Victory* was built. Our uniforms, some of which we make ourselves and others are made for us, the drill and weapons are all based on the regiment from the early 1800s up to the Battle of Waterloo in 1815. We participate in various re-enactments both in the UK and in Europe, organised by the Napoleonic Association plus other events organised from within by ourselves or by other re-enactment units or localities. We are proud of our living history, which aims to provide an insight into the camp life of a regiment of that period and we were one of the first Napoleonic groups to do this. This aspect of our group provides opportunities to people who may not want to portray the life a line infantryman, but will still be actively involved in the group using their own unique skills.

Contact

Email: the79thcameronhighlanders@outlook.com
Website: https://www.the79thcameronhighlanders.co.uk/
Facebook: https://www.facebook.com/The79thCameronHighlanders1815

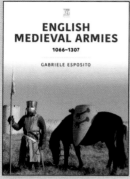
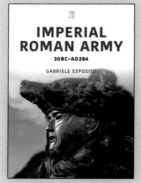
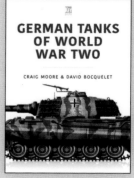
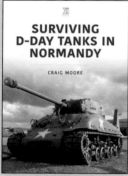
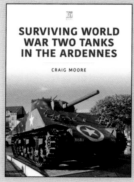
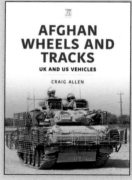